How Would You Like To . . .

- . . . forget that "exhausted" feeling at the end of the day?
- . . . get ahead on your job?
- . . . know the "biorhythms" that determine your ups and downs?
- . . . get more enjoyment out of life?

There's a "creative" way to approach every one of these goals, and many more like them. It's simple, it's natural, and it requires no great effort on your part—just a willingness to give your own innate abilities free rein. Dr. Erwin DiCyan explains how it's done in this informative and practical book.

CREATIVITY:

Road to Self-Discovery

ERWIN DiCYAN, Ph.D.

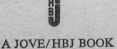

A JOVE/HBJ BOOK

First Jove/HBJ edition published February 1978

Library of Congress Catalog Card Number: 77-80713

Printed in the United States of America

Jove/HBJ books are published by Jove Publications, Inc.
(Harcourt Brace Jovanovich) 757 Third Avenue, New York,
N.Y. 10017

Acknowledgments

Writing is a lonely job for every author. Yet, digging into the works of creative people of the past and looking into as well as experiencing one's own creativity one has an immense amount of unseen company. Nonetheless, the seen company is the one that is palpably helpful to an author. And among those, I especially want to thank Miss Barbara Rogasky for the help that she gave me—for her judgment, and patience. There is a danger in any book that every comma can be in the right place but the spirit, modulation and humor have been gutted. She helped me in keeping those—even though in the process some commas are perhaps awry. And for repetition I make no apology—the same comments take on a different complexion in a changed framework. And that too, is a clear part of creativity.

Contents

PART 3

Foreword

By Walter C. Alvarez, M.D.

In my long experience as a physician at the Mayo Clinic and elsewhere, I often found that creativity can be a precious factor in diagnosis and treatment. Successful treatment of diseases is not merely a response to what laboratory tests have shown, but also how well the physician can interpret the findings among a number of variables. With the help of insight and intuition, often derived largely from a good history, one can get a good understanding of the happenings in the interior of a patient.

Years ago with the help of some sense of creativity I was able to shed light on the existence of little strokes, nonconvulsive epilepsy and several other, previously seldom-recognized, conditions. It has been said of me that I don't treat only diseases, but I like to treat people who have diseases.

For that reason I welcome Dr. Erwin DiCyan's wonderful new book on creativity. Because its contents are not limited only to details of medicine, it can expand the medical horizons of lay readers, and then by tapping their powers of creativity it can make a reader grow as an individual, a parent, a worker or a friend. It can help thousands of persons.

Preface

by **CHARLES D. ARING, M.D.,** Professor Emeritus
of Neurology,
University of Cincinnati, College of Medicine

For a number of years I was privileged to attend an ongoing seminar on creativity where persons of unusual achievement were dragooned into trying to explain how they did what they did. A thoughtful group called together for the purpose would meet, especially when a creative person came to town. Of course, there were a number of creative people resident in the city and on campus, and they too were tapped to lead such seminars.

These exercises were entirely fascinating and most enjoyable. What was invariably garnered was the setting in which an idea, formula, poem, book, musical composition, or the like was conceived but nothing of moment about the creative process. Indeed I doubt if it is possible for genius to tell how it operates. Freud was of this opinion and so too was William James, who said: "The cause and origin of genius are wholly inaccessible to the social philosopher; and if we are honest, we must accept the phenomena of genius as data just as Darwin accepted spontaneous variations."

Many creative persons seem to suggest that they are able to dip into their unconscious without loss of equanimity or equilibrium. They cannot describe how but their attem are highly engaging. Schiller's prescription was to " the watchers from the gates of intelligence." Shelley's theory of inspiration, much as Schiller's, was a sensibility that has no more dealings with intelligence than it can help. Coleridge spoke about "the streamy nature of association, which thinking curbs and rudders," and Wordsworth about "the widening sphere of human sensibility."

In contradistinction most ordinary people cannot spontaneously exploit their unconscious and maintain their stability. They cannot readily journey back and forth, but must maintain a more rigid psychological posture in which they feel safe. In this vein the Italian criminologist Lombroso looked upon genius as a useful form of insanity. But it seems that Salvador Dali comes closer to the truth with his terse self-appraisal: "The only difference between a madman and myself is that I am not mad." Of course, great genius can go mad and have done so on occasion just as their less creative peers. But as Lawrence Kubie* stated, creativity is not a result of neurosis but in spite of it.

I think we must agree with the noted contemporary teacher, Sylvia Ashton-Warner**, who said that the secret of our collective ills is to be traced to the suppression of whatever creative ability children possess. She described the mind of the five-year-old as similar to a volcano with two vents, one destructive and the other creative. To the extent that the creative channel is widened, the destructive is atrophied, and vice-versa.

Few have learned to use aggressive feeling constructively. Aggression properly modulated may be a force for good, or if misdirected it may be destructive. The uses of aggression are rarely learned at mother's knee, and the result is that many a lifetime is spent struggling with this energy misapplied. This not only warps the personality, it subverts the creative process.

I think there is little doubt that if we can shape a mileu hospitable to the presence of children as they are born every day, we shall have more genius. It is reasonable to act

* *Neurotic Distortion of the Creative Process,* University Kansas Press, 1958, pp 151
** *Teacher,* New York, Simon & Schuster Bantam Book, 1963, pp 191

upon the supposition that our crises and other problems as well may be soluble creatively. It was Goethe's opinion that "if children grew up according to early indications we should have nothing but geniuses." The self-interest of mankind calls for a more general effort to foster the invention of life.

It is perhaps not too late to try to restore the creative touch to the adult, whom Dr. Seuss characterized as an obsolete child. It seems to me that the main problem in fostering creativity is to maintain children so that they will not pass too quickly into obsolescence. Of late we have not been prone to suffer children gladly. Somehow we are inclined to prolong adolescence patiently and to deliberately defer maturity, in a process that short-changes youngsters at both ends. Our dedication would seem to be to submerge creativity rather than foster it. Dr. DiCyan's book is dedicated to put this to right—and also how adults can enhance their creative potential, which is within all of us. Too bad that it is suppressed by the social mores as we grow older.

Part One

Part One is concerned with a variety of topics, all of which touch upon creativity, and some of which are profoundly concerned with creativity.

CHAPTER 1

"We always are just the arrangers, not the composers, when it comes to creativity."
ZALMAN SCHACHTER

Parabola, Vol. 2; #2; Spring 1977, p. 87

What About You and Creativity?

Everyone has a potential for creativity. It is possible for everyone to enhance it, nurture it, to let it flourish but also to block or suppress it. If you are conscious of these conditions you will favor or facilitate its emergence.

And do not assume that the exercise of creativity is a mystical activity, food only for the genius. Mystical it may well be—because it deals with, or arises in the region of the unconscious of which we have much to learn. But is creativity a quality exclusive to geniuses? No. *Creativity is a democratic trait.* You and everyone else are all capable of it. You need but to develop it.

In this book, I will show you how to enhance your creativity.

Then, you may well ask, why it is that when I am given examples of creativity I hear only of geniuses mentioned, or other characters who went down in history—in fact, made history. The reason is simply this: the creative work of the characters in history is well known. You will more easily recognize it. It is creative people who made history—they are written about.

Ordinary men and women have made their lives happier, more productive, made their personal or social life more satisfactory—because they were able to rise to an occasion rather than "go by the book," and otherwise enhanced their interaction with people. Interaction with people is what success is all about in the social constellation, business, or other organizational activity.

Moreover many ordinary people in all walks of life who heeded their creative potential have created monumental names for themselves. That's the reason you hear about them. And that includes even Albert Einstein, who was a poor student at first, and finally landed a dead-end job in the Swiss patent office. Then, allowing his intuitive and creatives propensities to grow, he turned physics upside down. The world has never been the same.

Or, take the example of Heinrich Schliemann (1822–1890)—a successful businessman with a fixation. He believed that the city of Troy, famed in Homer's *Iliad*, had actually existed. The archeological establishment laughed at him. They even refused to publish a paper he wrote on that idea because, they said, he was not an academic archeologist, and was therefore not even qualified to have an opinion, let alone publish. But Schliemann was not discouraged by this hostility. Fortunately, being well-to-do, he had money to start his own exploration with the necessary equipment and hundreds of workers. Did he find Troy?

He found several Troys. One built on another! Fully excavated, these were cities with walls, streets, houses, neighborhoods, household goods, storage systems for water and grain, statues, weapons, and jewelry.

Schliemann changed our view of that part of the ancient world by his excavation of Troy (as well as Mycenae). His unerring instinct led him to an even more ancient civilization, Knossos, the old capital of Crete. He was right in assuming that the site he looked at was that of the ancient capital. That find would have been an even greater triumph—but he refused to pay the price of the land to excavate it. He haggled, but did not come to terms.

I am often asked how to recognize the creative personality. A creative person can be anyone. There are no benchmarks. But certain traits seem to be associated with them. Creative people are (1) more adventurous—they dare and are willing to hazard failure. They are more experimental and particularly curious to see "what happens." They do not automatically bow down to authority and so are often considered rebellious. (2) They are more spontaneous than other people because they do not fear to express an extemporaneous thought.

This spontaneity on the part of creative people is also partly because they don't suppress a thought. Many people fear to express an idea, wondering, "How-good-is-it?" and "How-will-I-look?" (3) Creative people appear to have more of a sense of humor, since many humorous situations result from seeing the old in a new way. (4) They have *and use* intuition and have the courage to express it. (5) They do not archly ask when faced with a task: "Is it creative?" Any task can be creative. People who say to themselves before undertaking a task, "I am worthy for creative work only" have a devotion to ego fodder rather than to creativeness which brings enduring, soaring joys to a person—and *genuinely* enriches the ego.

This does not mean that people who do not have these qualities cannot be creative, or conversely, that these qualities in a person assure creativeness. As with all aspects of human endeavor, we can type people only in bold strokes on a large canvas. But one quality distinguishes most creative people. They do not allow unfavorable circumstances—such as derision or discouragement—to stop them. One event which is conducive to creativity more than any other is failure to suppress a creative activity. Most people have creative potential but do not realize it because creativity is suppressed—by school, work, family. Similarly, creative people are said to be ill-tempered, easily irritated, arrogant, temperamental and neurotic. These are not traits of creativity *per se*—some people may have one or more of these traits and be creative *in spite of them.*

In the course of this book I shall try to answer many questions about creativity. And I will pose other questions showing you that the answers are easier than you may think. And you will probably agree, that there is more in this world than facts—or what we call facts. Attitudes can be more important than facts.

CHAPTER 2

What is Creativity?

What actually is creativity? It is the ability to see and construct an idea, a concept, which can lead to a wholesome or constructive application. It may be something that is quite simple, but it takes awareness or ingenuity to see it and apply it. Often, it is merely seeing the old in a new way.

For example, take Elias Howe, the man who invented the sewing machine. All was mechanically fine—except the idea of how to thread the needle so that it automatically fed from the spool of thread and in turn fed the material as stitches were made. Howe tried various ways but none worked until an idea came to him. He dreamed he was in the midst of savages ready to cook him. They had surrounded him and the ends of their penises were pointing directly at him—on which image he perfected the idea of threading the needle *not* at the head, which is the customary place where the needle is threaded, but at the point! Thus, the needle and thread could enter the material as it was stitched.

And nothing is too petty to respond to in a creative way. For example, the man who did more to reduce the deaths of infants and children in backward countries did so without inventing antibiotics or any other medicine. He invented the wire window screen. This prevented the spread of diseases by flies and mosquitoes. He cut infant mortality by 75 percent.

There are also other ways of defining or explaining creativity. One is the sudden and immediate recognition of the relationship between ideas and things. Another view: instant association leading to insight. For example, it is said that the *insight* into relativity came to Albert Einstein when he was a child. He had a childhood memory of being on a trolley, and as the trolley moved forward things outside seemed to go backward. Simple observation? Yes, things are relative. But this observation fermented in his mind for years and sprang up in the formation of his theory of relativity.

Other people have different definitions of creativity: 1. An understanding that comes to one, suddenly, clarifying a problem to which one reacts with utter certainty—in other words, an epiphany, which you know unmistakeably when you hit it, and in terms of the comics, an electric light bulb suddenly lights up. 2. An intuitive understanding of a problem even before the evidence for it is in. A German mathematician, Karl Friedrich Gauss (1777–1855), expressed it most succinctly: "I have known the answers a long time, even before I knew how to arrive at them." In other words, he was zapped by an insight.

A much better definition came from the British poet A. E. Houseman (1850–1936), who said, "Meaning is of the intellect—creativeness is not." He meant that creativity is not born of logic but of a deeper level, the unconscious.

But there are no hard and fast definitions of creativity, merely examples. You and I and the people around us recognize a creative idea when it is expressed. *Creativity has its soil in an intuitive foundation in which insight functions.*

Books have been written on the definition of creativity. But definitions do not perform a creative act. If you want a stimulant to help awaken the creativity within you, there is a comprehensive reading list at the end of the book. But I offer this caution: Sometimes we confuse the end with the means. When we do so, we get involved with the mechanics and overlook the soul. The objective is not to theorize but to move into the creative cast of mind. This is discussed throughout the book, especially in considerable detail in the chapters "How To Do It" and "What Not To Do."

CHAPTER 3

Creative People

What makes a creative person? He or she is characterized, by and large, as someone who looks at a commonplace problem in a new or different way. As a result he comes up, usually, with a solution that is most obvious—only after it is found.

For example, it was a creative person in a "think tank" that solved a problem facing the owners of a new building. Their problem resided in one bank of elevators: The passenger traffic on the floors served by that bank was so heavy that people had to wait a long time until an elevator came—in such a situation twenty seconds can feel like twenty minutes. They could not add another elevator because there was no room for the necessary shaft. The owners could not empty several floors of tenants to reduce the passenger demand because they would lose the rental income—an absurd idea. Nor could they switch another bank of elevators into service as the same problem would occur there—too many people and too few elevators.

The creative person came back with what seemed like an idiotic answer: install large mirrors in the hall where people would be waiting for the elevators. Did it work? Perfectly! People waiting for the elevators looked at themselves in the mirror, examined their own appearances, stole glances at the others around them. The elevators did not come any more quickly, but the waiting seemed to pass more quickly.

The creative problem solver is not wedded to customary

practices. He may have "way-out ideas"—which often turn out to be the solutions sought to certain problems. And he doesn't much care what people think of him. The creative person is not chained to the so-called "facts." These often turn out not to be facts at all, but customary beliefs and habitual ways of looking at things. For example, in the ancient world it was a "fact" that the earth was square and anyone who ventured out too far would fall off the edge.

Another quality is almost invariably applicable to a creative person—it is the intuitive leap. He has an intuitive *feel* for the nucleus of a problem, even before all the evidence is in on which he can base a decision, an intuitive quality present in all creative endeavors.

Another example of such an intuitive feel with no basic evidence is ascribed to Max Wertheimer (1880–1934), a German philosopher who saw a stroboscope in a toy shop. This is a device that rapidly exposes a series of successive still pictures so that it gives the illusion of movement when played back on a screen; motion pictures are based on that phenomenon. Wertheimer took the toy home, played with it, and leaped to the conclusion that you cannot separate the whole from its parts. From this idea he found the Gestalt school of psychology. The Gestalt school teaches, among other things, that to understand human behavior it must be studied as a whole, for when behavior is broken down into structural parts you are not studying the person, but only a part of the person. And the whole person is different than any of its parts. In other words, man's behavior is not a combination of reflexes and conditioned responses, but the sum of the responses.

Neither education nor intelligence is tantamount to creativity. Creative people are found in various types of endeavor, many of which lack the standard ideas of respectability. Old-time circus barkers or pitchmen are a good example. Usually unlettered con men, they were natural psychologists, often superior to public relations people in turning the minds of their public in the direction they desired.

Silk Hat Harry was most successful in selling soap by telling his audience that in ordinary soaps the fat comes from dead animals. Naturally this is so, for the tallow is rendered from the fat of animals—not stripped from live animals. Often reciting and emphasizing additional similar examples intended to provoke disgust, Silk Hat Harry extolled the purity of his product by chewing on a cake of his soap while giving his spiel, and in no time he sold out his total supply of soap.

A competitor of Silk Hat Harry's, however, bested him by lathering his hands and letting the lather dry before mounting the tail gate of his wagon to sell his soap. Then, he merely held his cake of soap in his hand and while water was poured on them the lather would billow down. The townsmen quickly bought out this huckster's line.

One needs no special expertise in one's profession in order to give birth to a creative idea. For example, we marvel at many of our civilized devices today—such as the universal use of lines painted on highways to keep the motor traffic in line and to prevent traffic jams. These lines have come into common use only within the last few decades. But painting bright yellow lines to mark lanes and to keep large crowds manageable was originally used in the eleventh century by Pope Urban X (1040–1099), who ordered them laid down for a celebration in Rome.

Another trait of creative people is the ability or habit of day dreaming, wool-gathering or reflecting.

August Kekulé, Swedish chemist, laid the ground for modern chemistry by coming upon the idea for the famous benzene structure—in a dream.

Society continues to give homage—often lip service—to creativity but does not gladly tolerate the creative person, who is often a maverick. It attempts to put him into the strait-jacket of conformity—he is much easier to handle that way. Teachers are probably the least tolerant of the creative individual because of the need to keep their classes manageable and to prepare their students for examinations. Creative kids are not usually the most manageable.

People often equate creativity with a high IQ. But though creativity may coexist with high intellectual capacity, it is not a prerequisite. The National Science Foundation sponsored a meeting of educators to consider creativity and to assess, broadly, the individuals who are likely to be creative. There was surprising unanimity of opinion on how we are starving the creative person in the U.S. educational system.

Two of the participants, educational psychologists Jacob W. Getzels and Philip W. Jackson, were studying the preferences and other traits of high school students. They found that the creative student puts a great value on humor, considering it first on qualities that he likes or considers important. The noncreative student places character first and humor last. The creative student is characterized also by his courage in taking risks to get into uncharted territory, a desire to get away from the stereotype and to go into a career that would meet his own standards rather than those that may be expected of him by family or friends.

Getzels and Jackson consider it a tragedy that our educational system tries to convert the out-of-the-usual-path student into conformity, and tragic as well its failure to recognize that the divergent traits of the creative talent are as important to society as the convergent talent of the stereotype of a good student.

Some problems that creative people met but surmounted: Michael Faraday (1791–1867) was an aimless youth and apprenticed to a bookbinder. But in that job at 13 he came across a book that had an article on electricity. That finished him as a bookbinder. Electricity was a revelation and possessed him, and subsequently he gave us fundamental developments in chemistry and physics.

Another unusual obstacle, built by a parent this time, is the one erected by the father of Blaise Pascal (1623–1662), French philosopher and mathematician. Trying to direct his son into the clergy, Pascal's father urged him on to study harder Greek and Latin and took away from him all books on mathematics which were dear to Pascal. Deprived of the subject most vital to him, unknown to his father Pascal developed his own system of mathematics. While he did not know it at the time he invented it, it turned out that by his own insight he reinvented the geometry of Euclid (app. 300 B.C.). This does not lessen Pascal's accomplishment—on the contrary, it reaffirms his unusual creativity for Euclid's contribution is one of the fundamental gifts that ancient Greece bestowed upon the world.

Creativeness resides in our everyday activities. We need to recognize it—being aware is the first step to recognition. One of the early recollections that many of us have is the ingenious way that Tom Sawyer had his friends help him paint a fence by making them pay for the privilege.

Possibly with that in mind, a woman who needed to have an old wooden garage knocked down used an equally ingenious device. Outraged by the quotation from a contractor for demolishing the tottering structure, she contacted a karate teacher, with the offer to allow his students to practice by knocking down her garage with karate chops. She also found a way of reducing her liability in the event of one of the karate students being hurt. She sold the building to the karate instructor for one dollar. This also enabled him to make a small charge to his advanced students for this extraordinary opportunity. In that way, she made him a subcontractor disposing of her burden of liability.

No job is too small to apply a creative twist and thereby increase efficiency. A maintenance man had to clean a very dusty basement from which previous workers had had to leave in coughing fits. He allowed hot water to run from the faucets and sprayed the air for the purpose of increasing humidity. (Dust particles coalesce in the presence of high humidity and fall rather than float.) After the humidity had built up sufficiently, he used a vacuum cleaner, further reducing the likelihood of raising dust.

For example, the perils of taking the Pill seem obvious. Shortly after oral contraceptives were introduced, reports of deaths from thromboembolism—clotting of the blood—started coming in. Yet, the need for oral contraceptives was a real one. How to get people to consider them? In some groups of people it is safer than in others.

One institution concerned with family planning sent out information that pregnancy has a much higher death rate than any known contraceptive, which is true. However, the older a woman the greater the death risk in pregnancy: when the figures were released that in the 35–39-year-old group the death rate from pregnancy is 5 times greater in pregnancy and in the 40–44-year-old group it is 10 times higher in pregnancy than from the pill the matter was put again into perspective. (The older the woman the higher the death rate both for pregnancy and in the side effects of oral contraceptives).

Creativity knows no bounds. Prisoners of war were able by their inventiveness to get a message across to the U.S. by a creative device. A prisoner of war was forced by his captors to broadcast a message to the U.S. stating how royally he and his fellow prisoners were being treated in their POW role. The alternative was punishment for him and his colleagues, with threats to execute every third man. The broadcasting POW gave a short and apparently spirited appreciation of his treatment. At the end he added, "Tell it to the Army, tell it to the Navy, tell it to the Marines. Also, let my friends in the U.S. know—tell it to Fats Jorgenson, tell it to Schwartz, tell it to Sweeney." It is commonly known in the U.S. that the phrase, "Tell it to the Marines," as well as, "Tell it to Sweeney," is vernacular for saying, *"Don't believe it."* Few foreigners know these expressions and that's how he got his message across.

Creativity knows no bounds in deed—and is fortified by observation. Hugo Zacchini (1898–1975) was a circus performer when he enlisted in the Italian army during World War I. He had plenty of opportunity to observe the trajectory of grenades and artillery missiles during field encounters. This gave him the idea of a human cannonball. When he returned to civilian life, he had himself shot out of the barrel of a cannon by compressed air and earned a good living the rest of his life.

CHAPTER 4

How To Do It

To become creative is really quite simple—and joyous when you see the results. Creativity is inherent within us, which we have as children but which most people lose in the process of conforming to the outside world and taking their place in society. Certain conditions must be observed, and practiced, to regain the creative potential.

COURAGE: A creative individual is not necessarily a talented one. Talent presupposes or suggests a methodological approach, a rational or historical precedent in an area in which a person is accomplished. For example, a man may have a great talent in finding out what is wrong with a piece of machinery and repair it. A creative person can perhaps show you how you can perform a given function without machinery. A talented person can write prose that is fine, clear and do it quickly, but a creative person can make it soar. It is more than a matter of degree. Creativity is more allied to genius than to talent.

Creativity means frolicking in territory new to most people, into which they are often initially fearful of treading. It is a willingness to open your mind to the unaccustomed—unaccustomed only because you may not have tried it. This book tells you what is needed and the steps you must take to do it. To enter an activity to which you may not be accustomed requires courage. It is courageous to take risks, especially when they transcend logic. Remember the example of the creative consultant who suggested installing mirrors in order to "speed up" elevators in a building?

Creativity also means involvement. If you feel something strongly enough and you have courage to try it, you are putting yourself on the line. It is only a passionate involvement in a cause or activity that will enable you to transcend the borders of what people call "common sense" and explore a creative solution.

Consider the difference between a creative person and an expert. The expert talks about what we do know and shares his knowledge with us. The creative person is concerned with what we don't know and thus goes into new territory. Courage means conquering fear, for fear is inhibiting. Fear may prevent you from seeing the old in a new way. Courage and passion can often transcend your ordinary way of thinking.

For example, it was such a creative leap that enabled Gutenberg (1400–1468) to invent the printing press. In his day they had the wine press, which squeezed the juice out of grapes. But Gutenberg was also familiar with the simple process of stamping a picture onto metal to make a coin. He saw the old—the wine press, the coin stamp—in a new way. How about pressing letters onto paper instead of pressing grapes, or pressing an image onto metal, using the same principle—that is, the wine press? In fact, when today we speak of the power of the press, we forget that that press originally was the wine press.

INSIGHT & SPONTANEITY: Seeing the old in a new way is using insight. And one insight creates other insights that can be developed. But you can destroy it by suppressing your spontaneity, by thinking what may be wrong with it, by trying to iron out all the wrinkles at once.

Spontaneity depends on insight, and intuition, and usually the creative person does not know from where or from what the insight sprang—except, that creativity favors the prepared mind.

The prepared mind includes knowledge of the subject in which the creative mind is involved. For example, if you are trying to solve a problem at work it is presumed you know something about your field. But it means more. It presupposes that your mind is not doggedly pursuing one path, closed off to any other. A dogged, rigid, methodological, analytic, rational approach that goes on precedent may well characterize a talented person—but not a creative one.

For example, French mathematician Henri Poincaré (1854–1912) came upon a solution of a mathematical puzzle by dropping the problem that deviled him altogether and turning his mind to another activity. The solution came to him—fully, suddenly, clearly, and perfectly—the next day!

In our Puritan culture we place a great deal of importance on hard work—if anything happens too easily it's not worth much. We feel a result that comes about without hard work is probably useless. *From a creative standpoint this is not so.* Listen to your inner voice. Don't suppress it. It may have the kernel of perception that gives you insight and may intuitively produce the answer. Indeed, it may turn out that you were wrong. But if you fear making a mistake you may also never have a creative insight or make a creative contribution.

CONSCIOUS "CORRECTION": Your conscious mind may be your greatest drawback to creativity. You must overcome its negating influence if you want to avoid the cautions, repressions, or inhibitions that accompany the conscious mind.

This does not mean that creativity is per se unreasonable or illogical, though often it is because creative solutions are often illogical at first sight. But the problem is that reason and logic often veil or cover a creative potential.

These so-called unreasonable or illogical forays arise from an unconscious preparation of mind. Remember that the conscious mind often suppresses or inhibits.

CURIOSITY: Basically, curiosity is a state of mind—it will stimulate your imagination, which in itself is a creative quality. Imagination in turn sparks an uncanny or unusual vision—in contemplating the alternative ways to a solution. In fact, the interest in an uncanny vision is one of the reasons (among others) for the resurgence of interest in the occult. Which is cause and which effect, I do not know, but it is apparent that they are associated.

Insight, one of the aspects of creativity is common to poets. In fact, insights are often prophetic. We know, historically, that many of the visions of poets have turned out to be right years later. In fact, creative people give answers to questions that have not yet arisen. For example, Freud's observation about a number of phenomena—which were prophetic—turned out to be true when they were clinically encountered.

Artists of various kinds, being creative people, are often prophetic in their visions. This is true of those who sketch, paint, and especially of cartooonists who devoted themselves to science fiction. Artists are ahead of history. Often they have vision in their forecasts.

Albert Robida (1845–1926) was a prolific French cartoonist who illustrated many classics, more particularly the early science fiction books. He illustrated them with war machines that did not then exist and drew aircraft, naval craft, and submarines that strangely resemble those of the 1970's. Creativity often is described as a look into the future, and Robida's work certainly fulfills that description. *Ideas spring forth luxuriantly from the imagination of artists before that of engineers who design and test that equipment.*

Other artists in 1932 depicted atomic war before it became a possibility. And in contemporary times artists did not lose their uncanny vision, which turned out to be prophetic. One example is the father of modern science fiction, Hugo Gernsbach (1884–1967) whose descriptions, if read fifty years later, could well have appeared in the daily newspapers.

I am not referring to such obvious common sense prophecies as "when a great number of people in the country have no jobs there is unemployment" which is ascribed to Calvin Coolidge (1872–1933). (This is parallel to similar observation who foretold that "if you spend all your money you will be poor." It may have been Benjamin Franklin, though he was an outstandingly creative person.)

Experience is universally prized, and it has enduring advantages. But in creative endeavors it is probably a hindrance. Experienced people know what cannot be done and therefore they are not fools enough to try it—and probably do not accomplish anything new that can be useful. An individual is often recommended because he is a *hard worker*. Indeed, he may be a hard worker but he may spin his wheels and assuage himself with the feeling that he worked hard.

But creative people have an almost mystical approach— the common-sense ideas of hard work and experience count little with them. They are usually broad in their variety of interests—a result of considerable curiosity. They are not highly structured in their organization but *hang loose,* allowing the stray thought to sharpen their perceptiveness, to give them insight, and allowing their intuition to range over a problem. Not being highly structured, they are not fond of the group-think called committees. At any rate, committees don't write poems. They have plenty of forecasts but little vision, which comes to the prepared mind.

The act of creation is like a hypnotic state—unstructured, loose, not fully awake, but certainly not asleep. What makes creativity difficult is fear. And creativity is easy if you allow your mind or feelings to wander into fantasy, which is probably expected as the creative mind is rich in fantasy.

This suggests that creative people are often given to reflection or daydreaming. This can be one of the most enduring gains in creativity. You can make your daydreams work for you. Dreams or daydreaming have been described by many creative people as precipitating a creative act, or preparatory to it.

Again, the Puritan ethic warns us against daydreaming. One of the complaints against school children is that they daydream in class. Such complaints by parents and teachers begin the societal suppression of the creative propensity in children.

Reverie. That is not the name of a nightclub or hotel in Miami Beach, though there may be one by that name. Reverie is a state of daydreaming, dreamy meditation of fanciful imagination. It is a method of hanging loose, emotionally and mentally. It is a state of letting your mind roam— and often in that process you may catch the measles of creativity. It is a symbol of an image more than it is of substance; but it is the substance of which dreams, or creativity, is made.

Remember the incident of Kekulé who solved the fundamental question of the benzene ring by dreaming of six snakes circled tail-to-mouth forming a six-sided figure? It was Kekulé too who laid great store on dreams or daydreams with his comment: "Let us learn to dream—then perhaps we shall learn the truth."

Among other creative men who were influenced by dreams are Sir William Herschel (1738–1822), the British astronomer who proposed the existence of the planet Uranus from an image in a dream; and Niels Bohr, atomic scientist, a founder of modern physics, who saw in a dream a mass of burning gas—the model of what happens in a change in an atom during atomic fission. Dreams are highly creative events.

Few people can paint highly imaginative pictures, or imagine a lyrical aura, or even the nightmare-like events in a dream. Probably for that reason many people favor painting landscapes or seascapes. But many painters and writers make it a point to remember their dreams as a nucleus of their creative work.

Dreams have untold riches—use them. They often anticipate actual happenings or give ideas on attacking problems. And everyone dreams, even though many maintain that they do not. The problem is to remember your dreams. This is not difficult to accomplish. To remember a dream do not open your eyes when you awaken. Verbalize it—out loud—with eyes still closed. Then repeat—with eyes still closed. Open your eyes, and while still in bed, write down the salient points. Following that write it out in some detail. Let no time lapse. Dreams are ephemeral.

The period between sleeping and waking is a most fertile one in which imagination can soar. It stimulates fantasy and creativity. Charles De Gaulle readily admitted that many of his plans formed during that period. Other creative people convert their dreams or the period during sleeping and waking into plays, novels or to give shape to other creative ideas.

While we cannot easily dream at will, we can daydream. It is a relaxing period that relieves tension and relaxes reins on the mind and spirit. It shuts out the conscious world with its distractions and tensions. In fact, often it is desirable to stop what you are doing to daydream; a creative idea may present itself. Such ostensibly aimless behavior may be among the richest of gains. Daydreams are pictures in the mind, with color, and sensual or emotional satisfactions. Reasonably sound people do not confuse daydreams and reality.

LOGIC: The logic of Aristotle has been the bedrock upon which the accomplishments of our world have been based. A thing either *is*, or *is not*; it is black or white. From that we derive a variety of things that limit and plague us, such as the conflicts between body and mind, God and devil, love and hate, good and evil. It polarizes our thinking and thereby limits imagination. Whether this is due to logic or despite logic is a moot point.

But one thing is certain: creative people have created works that often defy logic.

Sourian, a French mathematician, expressed creativeness eloquently when he stated that, "To invent, one must think aside." If one is not wedded to the yes-no system of logic one opens up alternatives (thinks aside)—a word that can trigger the solution of a problem. Nietzsche's comment, "The name is what makes a thing visible" applies here.

An example of aside thinking, or sideways thinking, produced the discovery of vitamins. In the early part of the twentieth century when research on various nutritional diseases was begun, the search was aimed at identifying a noxious material that might be responsible for a disease condition brought on by an inadequate diet or other influences. Casimir Funk (1884–1968), a Polish-French biochemist, took on a different approach. Maybe, he reasoned, it was the *absence* of something in the diet that brought on these anomalies? He was right—the concept of deficiencies applied here. He actually coined the name *vitamin*.

STAGES IN CREATIVITY: Inspiration can come without warning. But it usually comes to the prepared mind if it is receptive to creativity. Though creativity is suppressed when it is subjected to codification or other pedantic machinations, it has been observed and is generally agreed that there are four stages to the process.

Preparation. Here the conscious mind is concerned with or reflects upon a problem or a thought with which it is concerned. This could be in almost any endeavor—a way of solving a mathematical, scientific, or mechanical problem, such as fixing a motor or even home repairs; completing a literary plot, or planning a new approach to a business presentation; designing and cutting a garment from an idea in your mind.

Incubation. When one puts the problem or other concern aside, takes up another, an unrelated activity, the problem steeps in the unconscious mind; a solution may well be in the making. Again the example of Poincaré, who put his problem aside, went to the country for a few days, and concerned himself with other activities. He put the problem in his mind on *hold*.

Illumination. The solution springs forth suddenly, correctly, completely, during the time when the problem has been put aside to steep. The solution of his problem came to Poincaré as he was getting on a streetcar. While putting his foot on the step to board it he was "zapped" by an insight.

Verification. When Poincaré arrived home he tested the goodness or verity of the solution, and it was complete and exact, verifying that the stage of illumination truly brought forth the correct solution that he had long sought consciously but had been unable to reach.

These four stages appear to be extraordinary to the person who has not been involved in creative habits. But to the creative individual they are almost automatic; he dares, does not fear to be wrong, has developed a strong quality of inference—in other words he jumps to a conclusion sparked by a sense of inference.

Creativity is not a conscious brain endeavor. The brain is like a computer. It records automatically with mental beachcombing and therewith also takes on an overload of trivia. This beachcombing adds to the storehouse of information. Creativity in effect does the selection from the prepared mind, zeroing in, finding the proverbial needle in the haystack with an overwhelming impact, transforming it into the creative product. This is illumination.

Creativity can be observed all around us—at times in animals other than man. For example, as an experiment a banana was hung from the ceiling of a monkey cage that the monkey being studied could not reach. There were boxes all around the cage but not one was large enough for the monkey to climb to reach the banana. The monkey, in a creative burst, put one box on top of another and succeeded in reaching the banana.

The monkey's solution may seem obvious. But you must never overlook the obvious. It may be most satisfying and truly creative application. For example, the U.S. Treasury Department had a problem with one dollar bills, which, most in demand, wore out more rapidly than any other denomination. The solution did not lie in making dollar bills of stronger paper, which would break up the uniformity of the currency and thus make it easier for counterfeiters. The solution was to reintroduce the two dollar bill—in retrospect it is an obvious solution.

Often, we are blinded by seeing the obvious by the accustomed uses to which familiar objects are put, or even by their names; *names are associated with function.* For example, hammers are used to drive in nails or to loosen something that is stuck, like a window. But our accustomed means of looking often prevents us from putting common objects to new uses. For example, a hammer can be used as a lever resting on a fulcrum to lift heavy objects; or as an electrical conductor if the handle is insulated; or as a wrench, when two hammers are tightly bound together with wire.

When you are not tied to the accustomed way of looking at things, extraordinary ideas may well occur to you that no "reasonable" person would consider. For example: A man was planning a trip to Turkey. He wanted to buy various Turkish objects, but he didn't know how to bargain—he was a sitting duck. Turkish merchants intentionally quote higher prices because they expect their customers to haggle. If you don't, you may even deprive the merchants of part of the pleasure of doing business and you deprive your pocketbook.

Our traveler realized the need for bargaining in those circumstances. But he didn't know how; his meek attempts in antique shops were unsuccessful. Then he had the bright idea of trying an acid test. *He tried the U.S. Post Office.* While he did not expect to succeed, he would not feel that he failed as he had in the antique shops.

He went to the stamp window and asked for two 13-cent stamps for a quarter. The clerk looked at him with disbelief: "We have no specials—two 13-cent stamps are 26 cents." The man persisted and the clerk to get rid of the pest agreed, gave him two 13-cent stamps and took the quarter. Then the student of haggling was in a quandary. Being a creative person the idea struck him to keep up the bargaining lesson. "O.K., then give me 20 13-cent stamps for $2.50." While the Post Office clerk had been willing to put out a penny from his own pocket, he drew the line at 10 cents! While the creative stamp customer did not get a bargain sale at the Post Office, he did get a chance to practice haggling.

A lawyer who was a creative person assured himself of getting his fee for legal services from a good client, but one who had a penchant for a shrewd deal. One day the client approached the lawyer about doing a project that would be a long-term affair. That would have been agreeable to the lawyer, assuming that he would be adequately paid by that client. Instead, the client came with a proposition that would net the lawyer little, but the client importuned him to take the proposition and continued to praise him—what a brilliant man, and brilliant lawyer he was. The lawyer did not want to turn down that client because he was the source of fair income. But he could not afford to accept the proposition offered. An idea struck him. Referring to the client's flattery of his brilliance as a lawyer, he said, "Show me how I can be brilliant on your behalf and at the same time stupid on my own behalf by accepting the fee you offer." The client had no answer and paid the fee the lawyer asked for.

Incidentally, by and large, some lawyers can be creative people. But their training and mental programming is based on precedent—legal precedent establishes the rule. If your attention is exclusively on the past—precedents—you cannot easily attempt the unique solution that is without precedent. Usually, a creative act does not have a precedent in the same framework.

There are exceptions of course—the legendary solution of King Solomon. He decided which of two women claiming a child was its mother by ordering the child cut in half and offering each woman half a child. It was a brilliant piece of insight. The woman who was the true mother of the child withdrew, for rather than see her child cut in half, she would have let the other woman have it. (King Solomon in his judicial capacity apparently did not depend on precedent but on wisdom.)

People often wonder if creativity is a quality of the young and if it dilutes with age. Perhaps the pertinent answer is that creativity keeps people young in spirit, hence in body and mind, as there is really no clear dichotomy between the two.

There are many people in their seventies, eighties, and even nineties who are functioning well at their ages and are creatively occupied. The famous physician, Dr. Walter C. Alvarez, who was retired from the Mayo Clinic at 65, started a new career as medical columnist and author of a dozen books and is still active—writing and lecturing at 92. Grandma Moses only began painting at 88; Toscanini was still conducting orchestras at the same age.

Picasso, Goya and other artists were active in their nineties—their work is their memorial. Age is not a bar—only a creative attitude is needed for continued creativity.

Nor is a person too young to have creative solutions to what appear to be insoluble problems to other people. One day, a boy not yet in his teens was sitting on a fence at a country road watching cars, trucks, and horses go by. A large truck came down the road and suddenly came to a crashing halt just as it was entering a tunnel beneath an overpass. The overpass was too low and the truck too high. It was tightly wedged, unable to go forward or backward.

Men from the village soon collected and offered various means of moving the truck stuck in the tunnel. Many approaches were tried—none worked. The the boy spoke up. "Hey, why don't you let the air out of the tires and back up?" That lowered the truck, and the driver was able to back out easily.

It is quite widely held that the chance happening—the lucky break—is hardly accidental. It is rather the culmination of activities and thoughts that draw on the subconscious pool of sensations and experiences.

It was Pasteur's view that chance favors the prepared mind. When the sum total of information and sensations stored in the mind meets a problem, there may be a spontaneous, intuitive reaction that leads to a solution of the problem. Many believe that successful research—the kind that carries a *flash* or *spark*—is the result of that concatenation of problem and preparatory steps. It follows that the richer the storehouse of information and sensation, the more likely it is that a solution to a problem may follow.

To enrich that storehouse, it is possible to accumulate information and sensations systematically. It is also entirely possible that the deliberate, systematic acquisition toward accumulation will be wooden and will not lend itself to utilization—it may be an immobile reservoir. The mental storehouse is a fund of information, but there is a method to its accumulation—there is a *way* of thinking or of *arranging* the information to promote creative usage. A systematic and deliberate acquisition of information simply for erudition's sake may be too selective for creativeness.

But the acquisition of seemingly *useless* information becomes at times one of the most useful gains. Research is not limited to a mechanical screening of ideas but is principally the manner in which a curious mind arranges the wealth of material it has beachcombed so that it can retrieve, rearrange, or utilize it.

The variety of information in the mental storehouse controls to some extent the variety of the mind's inventiveness, or the variety of the problems that an inquiring mind can solve. A rich leaven of so-called useless information may create the very ferment that triggers a solution.

Retention of the fund of knowledge or information requires memory for its storage—and the ability to recall and to retrieve it. There is no gain in exposing oneself to a variety of experiences that one does not remember or does not integrate into one's frame of reference. Mere curiosity or experience then becomes useless. Memory does not presuppose that this accumulated fund of information is thrown together helter-skelter like clothes into a laundry hamper. Order is the first law of the universe. There is usually an arrangement with some indefinable nonconscious guilding principle, probably differing from person to person. The arrangement is not rigid or frozen into cells like an ice-cube tray, but has a kind of elastic classification. There is order in thinking, but this order need not be rigid. It is an order that *allows conveyance of information from one specialty into problem solving in an entirely different one.* In fact, one of the most rewarding experiences in research is the successful application of a method or a point of view from a strange or different discipline into one's own.

We should now examine some of the qualities that are attributed to the inquiring mind. One quality that is well prized is curiosity. Another is a broad and almost aimless interest in "anything." But curiosity by itself, can be idle, it may amount to not much more than gossip. Curiosity must take place in a framework of selectivity and of discrimination rather than by wanton garbage collecting or drawing from raw storage.

The practice of inquiry is not a ready-made craft to be learned in so many easy lessons, but one that is developed by an acquisitive and inquisitive mind, systematized by an orderly arrangement, and thus retained.

OBSERVATION & AWARENESS: We are the result of the sum of our input. Some of our input is aural—sounds we hear. Some is tactile—that which we know by the sensation of touch. Much or most of it is visual. These three basic senses are the instruments of our interactions with the world, including our actions and reactions regarding people as well as things.

It is understood that the keener our sense of observation, the more we will see and the more will be imprinted on our consciousness. And also the more or better we observe, the keener will be our understanding of the world around us and the greater the opportunities for finding or improving things—hence, the greater the opportunity to use our creative faculties.

Many discoveries in medicine were made by combining *observation with the creative ferment*. For example, the use of antihistamines to prevent seasickness was thus discovered. An allergist in Baltimore, Dr. Leslie N. Gay, prescribed such an antihistamine to an allergic patient. As the patient rose to leave, he casually told the doctor that this was the first time he hadn't gotten dizzy on riding to the office. A busy and nonobservant doctor would have just let the patient's comments go by—glad to get rid of a patient and see the next one. But Dr. Gay asked himself *a sideways question*. Would this product be useful for seasickness or other motion sickness? It proved to be so—the drug was Benadryl.

Another creative doctor who made the inductive leap and saw the old in a new way was Dr. Edward Jenner (1749–1823), an English physician who discovered the use of smallpox virus as an inoculation against smallpox. He had heard an old wive's tale that a milkmaid he knew was not afraid of getting smallpox—which was then ravaging England—because she had had cowpox. He thought of the relationship and began the use of virus from infected people for inoculations against smallpox.

Did you ever realize that the stethoscope was developed by Dr. René Laënnec (1781–1826) from an inspiration he received from two children playing near him in a park? He was sunning himself on a bench in a park in Paris when he noted that the children were playing with a long wooden plank that was lying on the ground. The child at one end of the plank tapped the plank sending a "message" to the one at the other end. This gave Dr. Laënnec an idea of putting a small cylinder of wood on a patient's chest and applying his ear to the other end. He tried it—and heard sounds no one had ever heard before. From this came the modern stethoscope composed of a flexible rubber tube carrying heart sounds from a person's chest to the earpieces of the doctor.

Other "accidental" discoveries in which a sensitive individual with a prepared mind observed a phenomenon and creatively converted it into a useful development: the use of nitroglycerine in angina pectoris which previously had been used only as an explosive; sulfanilamide as an antimicrobial agent which previously was used as a dye; an antifertility drug that did not work as such and became a fertility drug; metronidazole or Flagyl used for vaginal infections became a useful treatment for alcoholism. And consider the classical case of penicillin: Dr. Alexander Fleming, a British bacteriologist had some infected Petri dishes and was about to discard the experiment when he saw a clear zone around certain of the cultures. A clear zone means germ-killing power. He found that the contaminating *Penicillium* organism had cleared the zone— evidence of germ-killing power of penicillin.

But the way of a pioneer is not necessarily easy. More than seventy-five years ago a Chicago surgeon, Dr. Emil Riess, urged that patients should not be kept in bed for a matter of weeks after an operation but should become ambulatory in a day. He found that prolonged bed rest after surgery was usually responsible for pulmonary embolisms— blood clots in the lungs—from which most patients died. He observed the results of both long bed rest and early ambulation. But he encountered tremendous resistance because the new idea did not fit into the accustomed pattern.

Early ambulation finally became a common practice not because the establishment became more open-minded, but because during World War II a shortage of hospital facilities forced early discharge of patients to make room for new ones.

CHAPTER 5

What Not To Do

The exceptional person in any endeavor is often singled out, he meets hostility in various degrees. The creative person is usually a loner, though not in the sense of being a misanthrope but rather in the sense that he contributes best if left alone than as a member of a team. He rocks the boat. He makes waves. For this reason he is feared by management as a disruptive influence upon other workers or docile teammates. Management demands creativity as a lip service, but it looks upon the creative person with a general suspicion because it rarely understands him.

If you have an irrepressible creative urge and consider it more important than conformity and full acceptance by fellow workers you have to pay the price. Only you can determine if your creative freedom is worth the price.

But if you have decided to exercise your creativity don't be apologetic or defensive about it. If you feel something strongly enough, stick by it. You may well be right—and be momentarily celebrated. But above all, do not expect management to change permanently. (See Chapter 12.)

Also, don't avoid your fellow workers. You may not want to invite them to your house for a weekend, but you will do better if you are friendly with them and have at least token contact with them—as in company lunches or company picnics. In fact, you may gain—you may learn something or get an idea on which you can work.

While creative people do not naturally dovetail into the organizational pattern of most companies, you will also begin to realize that organization is a necessary device. Management has its responsibilities and can discharge them only in a structured, more or less rigid organizational pattern. The alternative is management by creative people. It has been tried. It does not work. But many companies are intelligent enough to realize that ideas—the lifeblood of a business if put into application—come from creative people, and they make allowances to enable them to work comparatively undisturbed.

Do not hold back in disclosing a creative idea that might sound ridiculous. If you feel strongly about your idea you'll have to chance ridicule—but it doesn't kill. Your "ridiculous" idea may become your company's treasured product. When you chafe under ridicule, say to yourself, "Get a horse." This will remind you of Henry Ford. He did not get a horse, his automobiles prevailed, and gained dominion. In fact, the best joke of April 1, 1898, was the purchase of the first automobile ever sold. Both the car and the April-fool joke backfired. But the car ran.

Above all, *don't be corrupted by common sense.* Everyone with common sense knew in ancient times that the world was flat. But Al-Beruni, born in Persia about 975 A.D., proposed in the eleventh century that the earth did revolve around the sun, and advanced the idea that there had been an Ice Age and also geological ages, which explained differences in climate and the reason for such phenomena as fertile lands and deserts. He was banished from Persia.

When you get a grand idea and it does not work just sit down to reflect. You may have missed an obvious point. For example, oxen were used as draft animals for centuries until some inventive primitive man hit upon the brilliant idea of using horses, of which a great number were available. Horses had many advantages—they were cheaper than oxen because only oxen were in demand as draft animals; and they were fleeter than oxen and also men. That creative primitive put horses into the ox yokes. It worked—for a while—but then the horses dropped dead. The ox yoke choked them. Whether he was disappointed that his idea did not work, or disturbed by ridicule he dropped the idea and nothing was done about using the horse as a draft animal probably for centuries. Then someone else in the fourth century probably sat down to reflect—why not make a yoke or a collar that does not choke the horse? Simple? The rest is history.

In fact, imaginative ideas to mitigate problems were in abundance in the ancient world but usually they were not carried far enough possibly due to lack of adequate technology. For example, the ancient Romans had the idea of a brake. They slowed their chariots from hurtling down hills by tying one wheel to the chariot so it could not move. It was then untied when the slowdown was not needed anymore.

Don't let the "scientific way" of doing things taint you. Ask yourself if your approach is objective, rational. It probably will not be if your creative spark has struck. Don't let them sell you a bill of goods—scientific, rational, or otherwise. If you have an outrageous idea, express it—especially if you have a *feel, hunch*, or *intuition* about it.

You may possible fall on your face—but you may soar. People often grasp at a tangible, rational explanation, have a Puritanical fear of soaring, and as a result they remain earthbound.

Don't ignore the obvious—it may have riches or answers. In a trial for damages by the survivors of an accident at a railroad crossing where a train crushed an automobile crossing the tracks at the same time, the key witness was a watchman. It was his job to signal a warning of the oncoming train. He was closely cross-examined: Had he been at the crossing *before* the accident? Where had he stood? Could he have been seen? Had he been sober? Did he have a lantern? Had he waved it? But the lawyer never asked the *obvious* question: *Had the lantern been lit?* It had not!

We tend to overlook the obvious by some mental device. In fact, the greater your fund of information the more likely you will be to think in the customary pattern and the less likely you will hazard or be open-minded. Don't read the label before use. If you don't, you may ruin what you are trying to do—which the label directs—but you may hit upon a superior method.

Don't discard a misadventure. That is how Masonite, the immensely useful artificial wood, came into being. Dr. Karl Mason was working to produce paper from wood fibers by a new, and he hoped an inexpensive, process. He was drying some experimental fibers, but since he had to leave for a few hours he turned off the heat, intending to resume the controlled heating when he returned. He did turn off the heat—but the valve did not work. As a result, he found upon his return that the fibers had baked into a smooth woodlike material. He was momentarily stunned. Paper? No. But since apparently he looked with an open mind, he realized that through misadventure he had come upon an entirely new discovery—artificial wood.

We have Bakelite because Dr. Leo H. Baekeland came upon a new type of material also due to a ruined experiment; he allowed it to heat too long and reaped a hard, almost indestructible mass—Bakelite. What happened? It started the plastics industry and contributed to environmental pollution. This discovery demonstrates the wandering mind may pay dividends greater than those envisioned by the original aim of the inventors.

And don't be afraid to play with words—an unexpected idea may strike you. In Grand Central Terminal in New York there was a florist's shop empty most of the time despite its excellent location. People taking suburban or other trains often buy flowers to bring home for expiation of sins or for other purposes; others send flowers by wire to a hostess after having been entertained for a weekend in one of the suburban homes. Normally it is an ideal place for a florist. But can you imagine who would send flowers to a sick person—or even a well person—from a shop called "Terminal Florist"? Had the florist allowed himself to reflect upon the word *terminal,* he would have seen that terminal means railroad station but that it also means the end. The shop closed down after being in business only a short time.

Similarly, don't react to words blindly. You may be misled. Words are usually loaded with meanings that prejudice confers on them. For example, few self-respecting businessmen or others involved in practical matters will welcome the word, "abstract," except in the sense of "to condense." But all of us are involved in practical matters. Why then react like a Pavlovian dog to the word "abstract," which is a practical symbol for such abstract terms as love, affection, loyalty, faith, hate. All practical events have a basis in certain abstract ideas. And the word "creativity" is an abstract symbol for a practical application.

Don't give a grandiloquent name to a group, society, company or other organization until you have figured out how it can be abused. A group disturbed by the general lack of curiosity among people formed an association that would bring their program to school children in the form of educational kits. A nonprofit corporation was organized and stationery ordered. Fortunately, the printer called the acronym of the name to their attention. It would have made the organization a laughing stock. The name was *So*ciety for *H*elping *I*nterest in *T*hings—SHIT.

Similarly, when the Nixon *C*ommittee to *Re-E*lect the *P*resident was formed, they would not have prevented the Watergate debacle but they could have saved themselves the public ridicule of being referred to as CREEP when that committee was being investigated.

Think beyond. One of the commands from creativity can well be applied to the above illustration. Don't stick to the pattern when it doesn't work. *Direct your attention differently.* For example, to reduce the increasing use of marijuana, legislation was passed to discourage its use. Nonetheless, use continued to increase—probably as a result of societal causes which legislation did not consider, let alone solve. To remedy that growing problem Draconian measures were instituted; the resulting severity was far out of proportion to the crime. This was an application of the same mindless pattern—with expected continuing failure. In New York State particularly, especially severe penalties were instituted whereby the penalties of infractions with respect to marijuana often exceeded that of murder or rape.

But if prohibition does not work, and there is ample evidence on that score, try an opposite tack: legalize marijuana. While its use cannot be stopped it can be immeasurably better controlled. Like gambling. And like prostitution against which senseless punishment is visited rather than an attempt made at solution.

Experts and False Prophets. If the experts had their way we would be dead, with respect to new ideas and growth in every sense. An alternative to creativity is a catalogue of wrong guesses, unimaginativeness, examples that surpass stupidities. It is enlightening to skim such a catalogue of sins, if for no other reason than to bear in mind that mindless obeisance to authority is deadly. And there are other reasons as well.

As late as 1945, Admiral William D. Leahy, who in the midst of the ferment of the new physics, and an *expert of course,* delivered this gem: "This is the biggest fool thing we have ever done. The atomic bomb will never go off, and *I speak as an expert in explosives.*"

Apparently, expertise alone is never enough when not fueled with imagination.

But you cannot very well fault Franklin Roosevelt in his forecast in 1922 because, then being the Under Secretary of the Navy, he was merely mouthing his party line rather than using his imagination: "The day of the battleship has not passed, and it is highly unlikely that an airplane or fleet of them, could ever successfully sink a fleet of Navy vessels under battle conditions." I wonder what the difference is between successfully sinking a battleship and unsuccessfully sinking it. During Pearl Harbor he learned otherwise.

Even Rear Admiral Clark Woodward as late as 1939 said, "As far as sinking a ship with a bomb is concerned, you just can't do it." And this was only two years before Pearl Harbor.

But let us go back a moment when the country was just beginning to grow—only thirty years after the War of 1812 with England. At that time, Henry L. Ellsworth, U.S. Commissioner of Patents, while marveling at our then *high state* of advancement (1844) looks ahead: "The advancement of our arts from year to year taxes our credulity and seems to presage the arrival of that period when *further improvement must end.*" (Emphasis supplied.)

At about the same time (1837) in Great Britain there was a similar prophet of doom, Sir William Symonds. He was an expert—surveyor to the British Navy. His simple myopia can well be the basis for a satire: "Even if the screw propeller had the power of propelling a vessel, it would be found altogether useless in practice, because the power being applied in the stern would be *absolutely impossible* to make the vessel steer." (Emphasis supplied.)

Watch out for pompous pontifications—some words that warn you in recognizing unimaginative, dogmatic experts and prophets are, *absolutely impossible, just can't be done, it goes against the facts.*

Impossible was also the word used to describe the result of the Wright Brothers' first flight. The brothers felt that as a result of their successful experiment of the flight of heavier-than-air aircraft, wars would become impossible. In fact, the French Peace Society decorated them—for had they not in 1903 invented the airplane, which would make wars *impossible?*

Outstanding physicists—perhaps outstanding in explaining what is known—quite often have tunnel vision. Were we to be guided by these experts with respect to a look into the future, we might not be regressive, but certainly static! Here is a look into the future by Nobelist Albert A. Michelson (1852–1931) pontificating when he dedicated the Ryerson Physical Laboratory of the University of Chicago in 1894:

The more important fundamental laws and facts of physical science have all been discovered, and these are now so firmly established that the possibility of their ever being supplanted in consequence of new discoveries is exceedingly remote. . . . Our future discoveries must be looked for in the sixth place of decimals.

Do not be intimidated—even by the majestic *New York Times.* In 1920 it characterized Robert H. Goddard, the man whose basic work made rockets possible, as one who "seems to lack the knowledge ladled out daily in high schools." They could not conceive of the possibility of rockets flying through a vacuum.

Some years earlier, a week before the first flight at Kitty Hawk of the Wright Brothers in 1903, *The New York Times* had had another lapse of imagination. It deplored the money that Samuel P. Langley (1834–1906), one of the early airplane designers, had spent in trying to fly: "Life is short and he is capable of services to humanity incomparably *greater than can be expected . . . from trying to fly"* (Emphasis supplied.)

But the most incredible argument against the airplane was advanced by an *expert,* chief of engineers of the U.S. Navy, Rear Admiral George W. Melville in 1901:

> If God had intended that man should fly, he would have given him wings. The airship business is a fake and has been so since it was started 200 years ago. Never has the human mind so persistently evaded the issue, begged the question, and wrangling resolutely with the facts insisted upon dreams being accepted as actual performance.

Most new ideas are at a variance with what is known as the "facts." Most of our so-called facts are merely *received information*—data offered as gospel with the hope that if it is called a fact, a belief becomes a fact. Again, if we would continue to depend on the experts we would be lost with respect to advances and developments. Experts who know all the facts are not open, apparently, to the practice of inquiry. Much like Professor Michelson (previously mentioned) their vision seems to be limited to pushing decimal points another place to the left. As to Rear Admiral Melville—apparently God had intended man to fly, but in his own way, beyond Melville's vision, who arrogated to himself the position of interpreting God's will.

Colonel Sir John Smith, an expert in warfare, advised the British Privy Council that bows and arrows were far superior in warfare than firearms. The reasons given were that firearms were more complicated than bows and arrows and could get out of order. Moreover, he said, "A bowman can let off six aimed shots a minute while a musketeer can discharge but one a minute."

This was 1591. Surely, no modern rifles were then available, but how about simplifying the "complicated thing" rather than staying with the bow and arrow?

Only about a hundred years before that, a commission had been appointed by Queen Isabella to study the feasibility of Columbus' proposal to find a new way to the Indies. She was intensely interested. As proof of her interest she appointed Hernando de Talavera, a scholar and her own confessor, to form a commission to study Columbus' proposal. After six years, the committee advised Isabella that if there were such a route, God would not have kept from the people a fact of such considerable value. And moreover, they said, that even if there were such a route, any learned person (expert?) would know that the waters were too hot to navigate. Nonetheless, after another two years Isabella outfitted three ships for Columbus.

Do not entrust your life to experts, they can often be deadly. During the Middle Ages, learned men—priests, judges, lawyers—were experts on witches. They tortured and executed what has been estimated to be hundreds of thousands of people. The experts in logic never saw the light that accusation was tantamount to execution. Torture was to make the accused confess. If he did he was hanged or burned; if there was no confession the accused died from continuous torture. Many of the accused named others they knew to be innocent only to get surcease from torture, which began again immediately afterward. Many accused admitted being witches in deference to authority: "I must be a witch if the judge says so."

Do you believe that such an acceptance of authority ended in the Middle Ages? No! In 1974 Peter Reilly, an eighteen-year-old boy was convicted of murdering his mother, in Canaan, Connecticut. When the case was reopened two years later, it was found that the boy had confessed to murdering his mother because the polygraph machine the police used "said" that he did. He even asked the polygraph operator for hints to supply details of the murder when the police pressed him for details on *how he did it.* René Dubos put it well: "A society that blindly accepts the decisions of experts is a sick society."

Perhaps this is as important a *don't* as any: *don't fear to be wrong.* The man who is never wrong is one who never does anything—wrong or right. Don't fear to be wrong if an approach turns out unsuccessfully, and don't fear to admit that you were wrong. You will increase your credibility with your colleagues. You will then be more easily believed when you insist you are right—creative people often have an unerring sense when they strongly and urgently feel they are on the right path.

Oliver Cromwell (1599–1658), English statesman, has a plea to his contemporaries that applies throughout the ages: "I beseech you, Sir, in the bowels of Christ, think it possible you may be mistaken."

A corollary: Don't fear to admit failure as a result of being wrong. There is one time only we must avoid failure—that is *the last time we try. We should fail to fear rather than fear to fail.*

Here is an example of a man with failures:

> Failed in business '31
> Defeated for Legislature '32
> Again failed in business '33
> Elected to Legislature '34
> Defeated for Speaker '38
> Defeated for Elector '40
> Defeated for Congress '43
> Elected to Congress '46
> Defeated for Congress '48
> Defeated for Senate '55
> Defeated for Vice President '56
> Defeated for Senate '58

That man was Abraham Lincoln—elected in 1860, sixteenth President of the United States.

CHAPTER 6

Factors That Enhance Creativity

Memory: In order to dredge up past sensations and experiences to utilize them for an endeavor it is necessary to recollect them—to remember them. And memory can be sharpened in a normal person.

Memory can be enhanced in two ways. One, is not to become fearful of forgetting, for in that way you program yourself to forget. The second, is to have hooks or pegs on which memory may be hung.

The second technique is called association. When you associate an event with one that is in your recollection, you will mentally hang it on the previous event and are more likely to remember it. And memory works through all the senses. How often have you recalled a past scene in the country when you smell fresh flowers, or a particularly delicious food you have had in the past when you taste it again—long after the original time. Smells are considered more powerful aids to recollection than seeing or hearing. In fact, Dr. Richard P. Michael of Emory University in Atlanta considers smells to be a powerful stimulant to mating behavior in animals—setting afoot a mechanism toward copulation in lower animals. These smells in higher animals are called pheromones. Research on the effect of odors in stimulating human libidinal or coital behavior is presently under way. (See Part 2, *Memory and Its Traces*.)

Accentuate the positive: A creative person is a positive person. A creative person takes risks—the risk of being wrong, of being derided usually by persons who do not have courage to risk or who cannot tolerate considering themselves wrong. Afraid of being wrong, these scoffers do nothing, to avoid that chance.

The creative person who first brought out the pocket watch—huge thing—was ridiculed. Every person in his right senses, he was told, knows that a timepiece that does not toll out the hours cannot work. And if it works, it is not reliable.

The affirmative stance removes the fearsome influence that negates. Moreover, how do you know you will not succeed until you try—again, again, and again? The time to fear failure is the last time you try something new.

Intuition & Insight: Intuition is the direct perception of a truth or a fact, without intervening reasoning used to derive it. It is the indefinable spark that suddenly gives you an insight to a problem or a situation. (See Chapter 22 Part 2, "Insight, Intuition and Intelligence.") How does it feel, I am frequently asked, when one is zapped by insight? The feeling is one of almost indescribable exhilaration—as if you are lifted into orbit and all mental and emotional clouds disappear. You have instantly tremendous sight—insight—and you wonder how you have missed the answer up to now. It is such a perfect fit! Many of the workers in creativity, such as Archimedes, Freud, Arthur Koestler, Abraham Maslow, and others have variously termed it the *oceanic feeling*, the *a-ha reaction*, the *peak experience*, *eureka* (Greek for *"I have found it"*). The legend that Archimedes, to whom the idea suddenly came in a bathtub of the method of determining the volume displaced by solids, ran naked from his bath through the streets shouting, "Eureka," is entirely plausible and credible.

Insight is the wisdom of the soul. It comes to the prepared mind, not as the result of hard work but through intuition, leading to the indefinable stroke of insight. Insight is the nonverbal cognition of relationships, including putting familiar things in a new arrangement. For example, traditionally, only the wealthy could afford to ride in a horse-drawn carriage up to the eighteenth century. The poor walked from town to town or lumbered along in a horse and wagon. However, in about 1660, Blaise Pascal (1632–1662), a French philosopher invented the idea of an omnibus, a large horse-drawn vehicle with at least thirty-five seats. Seats were available at a modest fare so that the poor could ride long distances.

Was not that an obvious development? It looked obvious only after the idea or insight struck Pascal. Subsequently it developed in a variety of forms and uses to the present-day buses, trains, and railroads that anyone who has the fare can use. And one does not need to own a bus, plane, or railroad in order to use it.

Intuition means *not going by the book*. The individual who is considered *a stickler for details* goes strictly by the book, thus screening out his imagination and fortifying his fear of soaring or of allowing his feelings or hunches to prevail. Usually, his hunches atrophy—he has successfully suppressed them. Such an individual goes by the book as he fears to trust himself or his inner capacities. He truly may have none left.

For example, a given lady rose from secretary to managing editor for a medical journal because she knew by heart, backward and forward, *Robert's Rules of Order*. This came in handy in meetings of the society that published the journal. In that way she supported her boss, the editor-in-chief, who was a sterile man and welcomed not having to rely on judgment—using *Robert's Rules of Order* instead. But at times situations arose—as they will in an organizational setting—where judgment has to be applied. When these two were in a situation where judgment or a spontaneous response was necessary, they fell apart.

Humor and Games: Humor is a creative act. Surely, when you see the old in a new way you are creating a new situation, often spontaneously. In his outstanding book, *The Act of Creation*, Arthur Koestler gives an excellent and amusing example.

An art dealer bought a painting by Picasso, then brought it to Picasso and asked him if it was genuine. Picasso after looking at the picture said, "It's a fake." The art dealer was deeply disappointed, began to doubt his own judgment, and left in a downcast mood.

Some months later he bought another painting done by Picasso. While he was sure it was genuine, nonetheless with the memory of his previous experience, he went to Picasso again, hoping to be confirmed in his view that it was genuine. Picasso looked at the painting and said emphatically, "It's a fake." "But I saw you working on that picture. How could it be a fake?" asked the astonished dealer.

"I paint fakes too," answered Picasso.

It takes creativity to see the old in a new way, to see an unexpected relationship. Often seeing such can be humorous as well as creative.

And humor, it is said, "Is not a gift of mind but a gift of the heart." Most contrived humor—cerebrated by the mind—usually falls flat. It takes spirit to see or produce the outrageous situation, to change the focus away from the expected. It is the sense of the ridiculous, the ability to laugh at oneself that the spirit suggests. Probably for that reason people who genuinely laugh readily and see the humor in situations are more open and approachable. Humor can also be used, usually at someone else's expense, as a form of hostility. This, however, is readily discernible to the sensitive person.

Creativity is often a change of focus from the expected. Humor frequently utilizes the change in focus from that customarily expected, producing an unexpected often ridiculous situation that is frequently highly amusing.

For example, a man told his friend that he was suffering from hemorrhoids, which discomforted him greatly. The friend told the sufferer that he'd heard that club soda was excellent for piles. Some weeks later the two men met, and the friend who had suggested the remedy asked the sufferer how the club soda worked. "Terrible," he was told. "It almost killed me. I needed an operation after using the club soda."

The friend was surprised. He wondered what happened. "Were the bubbles too strong when you used it? What happened?"

"How am I to know about the bubbles?" answered the sufferer. "They were still in the bottle when I inserted it."

Humor has another dividend. A psychiatrist once said that he never had to treat anyone who could laugh at himself.

Closely related to humor are games or toys because they are devised to give fun. But they are also a marvelously creative instrument for everyone, especially for children. Even for adults, toys are a fountain of goodies as they enable the user to see things in an unaccustomed way. That can carry over into real life, and it's a habit of creativity. Unfortunately people do not take toys seriously because the word *toys* calls forth a signal or symbol that is denigrating to the "serious" person.

Toys and games give people the opportunity of using creativity in arriving at the objective. But experimental games not accompanied with directions for playing them oblige the players to infer what steps to take or how to take them toward a given end. This stimulates the creative propensities even more. If the objective is stimulating creative potential, winning is unimportant. In fact, in the competitive heat much of the creative potential is lost—if winning is the sole aim. The objective of games should be relaxation. If competitiveness is at the heart of the game, then the difference between games and the daily competition becomes obscured.

Relaxation: Everyone has met the man or woman whose pride is *working hard and playing hard*. In our Puritan-oriented culture, working hard seems to be an end in itself. How many times have you heard a man described as a hard worker, with no comment on how effective or wise a worker he is? It appears that working hard or doing hard tasks—no matter what—becomes an end in itself. It is a clear confusion of the symbol with the object.

But being creative is not *hard*. That is probably one reason for the suspicion with which creativity may be viewed. It does not appear to be manly because you don't work hard at it, yet while not hard in the common sense of the word, it requires certain preparation.

One of the most important conditions for creativity is relaxation. It is not merely relaxation of body, but relaxation of mind as well. Many people do not know how to relax—or have forgotten since they were children, when they would daydream.

There are several ways of relaxing. One is to let the mind wander, allowing oneself to indulge in fantasies or in daydreaming. One cannot force it. One cannot work hard or play hard at it. Unfortunately, our culture also does not take kindly to daydreaming. Children are discouraged from it.

Daydreaming or allowing fantasy to roam reduces the overloaded sensory input and allows the mind to look into itself. It slows the metabolic rhythms of the body. Heart, breathing become slower, and even the brain waves are altered to a predominantly alpha rhythm, which is associated with relaxation or relaxed concentration. One does not fall asleep but is awake and rested. It increases sensitivity.

But don't work or try to work too hard to relax!

One form of relaxation that is eminently successful is transcendental meditation. The use of a *mantra*—a meaningless syllable—enhances meditation through concentrated attention on the mantra. Distracting thoughts are filtered out. People who practice TM ® arise from a fifteen to twenty minute session relaxed and refreshed.

But do not depend on TM ® or other forms of meditation to become creative. They merely give you a method of splendid relaxation, relaxed awareness, or a relaxed state that is conducive to creativity. Certainly, one cannot evoke a creativity-conducive cast of mind by excitement, by frenetic working hard and playing hard.

Relaxation and rigidity have only one thing in common—the first letters of both words. Otherwise, they are antipodal—at opposite ends of the spectrum. To relax, *hang loose* metaphorically: that is the opposite of rigidity. (See Chapter 16, "Meditation, Transcendental or Otherwise," also Appendix "What Are We Living For," and "What Does One Do For Fun.")

Feeling Your Way: It is said that 10 per cent of all people think; 20 per cent think they think; but 70 per cent would rather die than think.

In the above paragraph try substituting *feel* instead of *think*. When you dip back into your memory, you will no doubt recollect that comparatively few people feel, perhaps a greater number believe they feel, but that most people would rather die than feel or express feeling—let alone be comfortable in expressing it. Predominantly true to men, it is fortunately, in a much smaller measure, also true to women. And feeling is strongly associated with creativity—which we will soon discuss.

Have you noticed how comparatively few people mention the name of the person to whom they are speaking when talking to someone, personally or by telephone? Have you noticed, too, the distance at which people stand when speaking to each other? It is as if they fear the invasion of their territory. Why and what are they protecting? Probably they fear awakening feeling or of responding to feeling.

One can simplify again and put the business of impediments to expression of feelings into two kinds: (1) those who can feel but cannot express it, and (2) those who articulate or express it but do not feel.

Among those who can feel but cannot express it are people who may have a warm, affectionate or even loving feeling for another, but more often their center is on themselves. They have a need for those warm, affectionate, or loving feelings, which they would like to receive, but are mute verbally or by nonverbal communication. They cannot send a signal of their need and find it even more difficult to express. It is as if, were they to express it, they would "lose control" of themselves. They are unaware of the phenomenon that surrender often means victory. Their propensity for committal is virtually nonexistent. They find it even difficult to express a compliment to others, for in their hearts it requires giving up a part of themselves.

Such people, emotionally immobilized, usually find creativity difficult because creativity demands taking a risk, giving part of one's self. It is like taking an unaccustomed step—a risk—a fear of rejection. An unsuccessful attempt can be construed as a rejection, which such people fear. Perhaps they have had many examples of rejection from their own family or from peers when children. They fear taking another risk. They have not yet transcended this fear, nor learned to give as well as receive.

The other group—those who express but cannot feel— are perhaps further from feelings. These are usually articulate people who cover the void in their feeling with astute verbalization, giving the appearance of sincerity, the cloak of involvement. Often they are all for humanity and society but shy away from personal involvement with people because in that area they are empty. Excellent examples of these two types—not uncommon traits—will be found in an engaging book, *Autobiography of My Mother,* by Rosellen Brown (Doubleday, New York, 1976) *(See* Chapter 14, Getting Acquainted with Your Emotions"—and Chapter 17, "The Sixth, Seventh, Etc. Senses.")

Conformity Vs. Nonconformity: In the 1960s the flower children or hippies, rebelled against conformity—as most younger generations do. It is in itself a learning process, a daring process, a trying out of wings to be able to fly under one's own power. But while they dropped out of the various restrictions of conformity, they set up a style of conformity all of their own.

What is the difference whether you are enslaved by one master or another? Would they, who cast off the shirt and tie, dare to be seen among their fellows in other than tattered blue jeans? Would they have the courage to toss off that uniform?

Conformity or nonconformity are not external traits. The external clothes do not produce the independent, curious, questioning state of mind that is associated with the creative personality.

At times people become opponents to an idea—any idea—for therein they believe they demonstrate their superiority. Similarly, people also use another ploy: They may try to distinguish themselves by doing "something different" merely for the sake of difference. One form is an intentional show of nonconformance to set themselves off and apart from the "average guy."

If such people were to put the effort into increasing their substance that they often do in giving a show of superiority by their nonconformance, they would have more substance than fluff, which their attempt at nonconformance shows.

Nonconformity is not necessarily a trait of a creative person. It may well be, and often is, a result of their other activities (solitude, reflection, curiosity, etc.) that makes them different. But it is not a planned program—when it is present, it is usually a result of other creative traits.

Symbols, Metaphors, and the Literal Trait: Some people are quite literal. They do not know how to take others unless the action is very straight. Literal people often have a weak sense of humor—probably because a humorous remark or incident requires a different focus and cannot be taken literally. While literal people can be imaginative and are often highly capable in certain activities—as they put direct effort into activities in which they feel safe and unthreatened—they suffer certain deficiencies: One of these is the deficiency of the metaphor.

Literal people cannot see a metaphor or do not utilize it. They take it literally. They do not trust their judgment in weighing it or evaluating it. The use or understanding of metaphors takes imagination to put it in its proper place. Some metaphors are universally understood, such as, "It was raining cats and dogs." Other metaphors require an imaginative leap in order to comprehend them, such as, "Words are a device, but they are even more an environment." That is, the words people use not only express their ideas but they also establish the emotional climate in which people think. (*See* Chapter on Myth and Metaphor). In any event, it is a creative facility that is at play in the making of a metaphorical statement and often understanding its purpose or value. Metaphors strengthen a verbal picture and expand it.

Closely allied to metaphors are symbols. They are metaphorical in a characteristic way and often their interpretation requires particular knowledge or a strongly creative leap.

What use are symbols? They are part of the nutrients for the soul. They appeal to our emotions, not only to our intellect. And the role of the spirit or soul—or by whatever variant it is called, such as intuition, or insight—form the building blocks in erecting the edifice of creativity.

Symbols also have a deeper meaning—they are the shorthand of the language of the soul. For example, the staff carried by a bishop, the crozier, is a symbol of his office or function, as a shepherd of his flock. The crozier is a stylized version of the shepherd's staff.

Symbols serve other purposes too—as reminders. For example, the power over life and death was symbolized in Roman times by the lictor—the bundle of rods and an ax—found also on U.S. dimes minted before the 1960s. Today it is used as a symbol of governmental authority, though its power has been curtailed by English law since the Magna Carta. Unfortunately it was brought to its full meaning by Mussolini's Fascist armed squads during his short dictatorship.

An example of a literal-minded person: A farmer was grazed by a bull and was hurt. His insurance agent in making out a report described the event and called it an accident. The farmer refused to sign the report, which was request for compensation, because he said, it was not an accident, "the bull meant it." Another literal-minded person was told that a guest he invited could not come due to illness and besides, said the guest with a twinkle, "If I came I would probably ruin your dinner party." The literal-minded host replied: "Why do you say that? Do you expect to start a fight during your visit." The host was not aware that the guest's comment was either a joke or a bid for a desire to be reassured that he is welcome. (See Appendix, *Myth and Metaphor*)

Articulateness: Creativity is the process of the development of ideas. Communicating ideas is another thing. While creative people are often articulate, they need not be to be able to utilize the ferment that foments ideas. But often people confuse the idea of creativity with articulateness much as they confuse fertility with potency. These are two different functions.

If you are not particularly comfortable in expressing yourself or are not as articulate as you would like to be, it will not prevent you from enhancing your creative potential. Articulateness is indeed a desirable quality: It enables you to convey ideas to others, to induce them to accept your ideas, to exchange ideas—in short, to communicate. In fact, communication is what interpersonal relations is all about. But if you are not articulate it just means that you have difficulty conveying your ideas; it does *not* mean that you do not have a creative potential.

CHAPTER 7

Boredom

It was mentioned before that boredom (and its often accompanying depression) are much associated with our civilization. (According to a World Health Organization estimate, 3 to 5 per cent of the world population of 4,000 million, suffers from depression—an equivalent of 120 to 200 million depressed people, disclosed at a 1976 symposium on depression in Lucerne, Switzerland. Boredom is particularly prevalent in more or less affluent countries. You don't get bored when you have to strain all your resources to scrounge for food—to stay alive. Boredom is the virus in our culture that breeds sickness of soul, then of body.

When the magic of our lives has evaporated, we try to replace it with various sensations in the hope of recapturing it. It was the ennui of the Romans during the latter empire that threw Christians to the lions—a sport to relieve weariness or boredom. It is probably the boredom of hoodlums, due to the lack of inner resources—that attempts to overcome their discontent, that precipitates thrill killings—from one thrill to another, in an escalating series of outrages. The boredom of that subculture arises from a psychological emptiness, and from a lack of commitment to work, or to a person, or to some gainful activity. The Sunday blues, the empty weekends, similarly attack people with few inner resources.

Children get bored. Their early lives are often full of boredom punctuated with frantic activity. The phrase of young children, "What shall I do now, Mommy?" is clearly a plea to help alleviate boredom. While Mommy can suggest activities, children soon tire of them. Their attention span is short, they soon tire of a new toy. Continuous input is sought—and necessary.

Our brain cells need certain foodstuffs to function, to stay alive. Preeminent among them are sugar (glucose), oxygen—*and intellectual activity*. Chemical transactions take place in the brain during every moment of our lives. During waking periods some of the transactions that take place result from mental or intellectual activity. It is the input that the brain needs. And active rather than passive input is desirable. For example, if your input is customarily passive, as a spectator, you will often fall asleep. Boredom during a TV show often puts people to sleep. We go from one boredom to another. While this falling asleep does not have the side effects of tranquilizers, it does have a side effect of its own, perhaps one as destructive. Boredom puts you to sleep and in the process kills perhaps thousands of brain cells.

We have about 10 *billion* brain cells. Naturally hundreds die every day, and with even moderate drinking their rate of destruction is hastened by lack of input. Lack of any input can make you go out of your mind—literally speaking.

The brain needs continuous input for healthy stimulation. With the flatness of our emotions, we look for external input of all kinds. As expected when there is no rich emotional matrix, we seek trivial input.

And what input does the average person seek? TV, movies, and sports events assail our senses. Note that all of these are passive activities, and in addition they dull the mind. So ever stronger stimuli are necessary, also to make up for brain cells that literally die from lack of active stimulation. Our judgment of values becomes clouded. Perhaps that is one of the principal reasons why retirement often spells death—due to boredom.

One of the reasons we need change is because it stimulates. Does this mean that you should take steps to scrape for survival—to prevent boredom? Not at all recommended as an alternative.

How do you get out of that rut? How do you find options less deadening than TV is to you?

Creativity is just such an option. It is the antidote to boredom and, simply, if you are creatively engaged you will not be bored. Boredom and creativity are antithetical—two extreme ends of a scale. Since you probably cannot jump suddenly into creativity, you can prepare for becoming involved in it. How? By changing liabilities into assets.

For example, awareness, sensitivity, perceptiveness, involvement—especially by sharing—are all related to creativity. Use these even through the options available to you—as TV. Spending time before the TV set and then turning yourself off when you turn off the set is admittedly nonconstructive. But if that is all that is open to you at this stage you can turn this liability into an asset by becoming involved, communicating.

In other words, *by sharing it,* by communicating with others even if you have to use people as a sounding board. By sharing is meant more than retelling the story you just saw on TV. It means that by giving your views, feelings, interpretations and extrapolations, by eliciting and inviting the view of others, other events are affected.

There are many advantages to sharing. One is mobilizing your ability to become involved—a tremendously effective antidote to alienation. Another important dividend to sharing is stimulation—when you share, there is also input. It is assumed that sharing is an exchange of ideas, not a monologue by you.

And sharing, exchanging, intercommunicating will make you a better observer. As you observe more, you will have more to share. And you will enrich your storehouse of experiences, sensations.

Since you will be sharing, namely giving and taking, you will be making memories. You make memories by recollecting your experiences of exchange with others.

And do not worry about forgetting. Memories are not lost. For example, under hypnosis, old as well as comparatively recent events are clearly recalled, evidence that the tape of memory is not erased, only covered over. So do not worry about remembering or forgetting; whatever you put into the memory bank helps generate the next creative idea. In making memories you increase your storehouse of sensations and experiences. In short, you increase your storehouse, your psychic reservoir.

But exchange means give and take. Listen—as well as talk. Unfortunately many people do not listen to or hear the person to whom they are speaking. The wheels in their head are working furiously, planning what clever remark to make in answer before the other person had even stopped talking. It is said that the reason many people listen is that they are merely waiting to be able to speak. That is not exchange. Better listen—you may learn something. (See Chapter 24, "Memory and Its Traces; and Appendix, "Poetry and Creativity" and "What Are We Living For").

Observation: Observation enriches you, both with facts as well as impressions, which are often impalpable. These intangibles are often at the fountainhead of creativity, which deals with perceptions, intuition, and sudden illumination. The more you have the more you can draw. But to add to the storehouse—both facts and impressions—you have to sharpen your observation.

How do you sharpen your observation? By looking, yes. But that is not enough. An unimaginative person looks at a building and he sees nothing but the bricks and mortar of a large office building. But what does the building house aside from offices? Have you noticed that whenever you pass a certain office building you see young men with long hair and knapsacks either coming in or leaving the building? They commonly carry nothing in their hands—it could be that a messenger service is in the building. Does it excite your curiosity to find out what these oddly dressed people are doing there, or what is in the building to which they gravitate? Did you ever ask one of them? Or did you follow one into the elevator and see to what office he was bound? You were not curious?

Curiosity is one of the traits of the creative person.

Do you want to sharpen your sense of observation, exercising one of the traits of a creative person? It is simple enough to do both. Make a mental scenario accounting for the young men you saw coming or going at that building. You will also use your imagination doing so. Add some possibilities, such as girls. How do you envisage them to look?

Make several such mental scenarios, with different events and endings. You can only exercise or practice something by doing it.

If you construct these scenarios a building will no longer be merely a pile of bricks and mortar. You will have vitalized things—you will have created events. That is one of the things creativity is about. It will engender a creative habit with you.

You will be a step nearer creativity. And creativity is a continuous and perhaps never-ending process. You cannot exhaust it.

Nothing is too petty for creativity: You may still be laboring under the misconception that creativity means creating a painting or a musical composition. It includes such things, but it is not limited to them. Since creativity *per se* will give you tremendous satisfaction, nothing is too petty through which the creative facility can be expressed—and greater creative activities can follow. Creativity follows upon creative activity. It is cumulative. There is a *joy in creation* and the nature and size of the creative act does not really matter. When we think creatively and follow up our thinking with creative acts, we continuously expand our creative ability.

For example, the man whose fuse blew at night and had no other fuses but bridged the contact by putting a penny temporarily in the fuse box acted creatively. That is not what pennies are used for. What he did was to rearrange familiar objects into a different constellation. Creativity is that too—rearranging the familiar in another setting or constellation.

There are thousands of such examples in which creativity can be applied. The more you use it, the wider will your vision become, and the broader will be your area of application.

One caution: never say, "It cannot be done." Because it *can be done* when you free yourself of the accustomed practices or ways of thinking. For example, you have storm windows and the window glass broke and needs replacement. The broken storm window cannot be removed by pulling it out through the inside, which is the customary mode of removal and replacement, because after it was installed window bars were put in. The window bars are riveted into place. Removing then replacing them would weaken the anchorage they have to the integral window frame. The broken storm window cannot be removed from the outside, as the outside tracks made the window smaller, and the broken storm window will not go through. Several glaziers, experts in window replacement, said it could not be done—the window glass on the storm window could not be replaced.

But it was done. And quite simply, by unscrewing the whole storm window frame from the outside by removal of the screws which held it to the outside of the window frame.

Inhibiting Factors: The expression of creativity is perhaps as much a function of taking away as adding: doing away with factors and influences that inhibit it, rather than forcing creativity to grow. You need not force it; you need only to be aware of creative traits and use them. Above all, do not inhibit the expression of creativity.

Creativity is inhibited in many ways from childhood on. Children are told to "go by the book." They are discouraged from daydreaming. People are urged to do things by the "tried and true" method. Workers are discouraged from trying a new way—they are told to follow custom. People are importuned always to read directions on labels even if no question of safety is involved. People attach function to the name of an object and so limit it. But if everything were done by looking at precedent there would be no advances.

Further discouragement against trying a new approach is

fear of cost. When estimating, people use the figures of their experience—which is, naturally, a sound basis for determination of a fixed cost. But isn't it possibly more profitable to try to find a less expensive or more efficient way? All progress is based on that philosophy. Investments in ideas have paid off in the long run.

CHAPTER 8

Science: Logic Becomes Illogical?

Our cultural heritage venerates logic given to us by the Greeks and embellished by philosophers during subsequent centuries. The scientific method is based upon logic as a fundament, or as a party line, depending on what you wish to accomplish or what objective you have in mind. All activities in technology and other endeavors require rigid logic as an instrument for attaining the objective.

But many creative leaps are not logical to begin with. The inductive leap springs from an amalgam of the following: intuition generated in the unconscious and steeped in intangible though real sensation; it does not follow the orderly logical procedure with which we are all familiar. It does have an order all of its own, allowing cross-fertilization through certain steps—preparation, incubation, illumination, and verification—discussed in several other places in this book. The inductive leap has a logic all of its own.

This is the reason for the need for relaxation—to disavow the otherwise necessary rigidity of logic; and also the need for feeling rather than thinking, in connection with creativity.

The point is: Do not worry if your trek through the unknown land of creativity is not logical. In fact, that is the point. It is a different language. And above all, don't fear—especially don't fear ridicule. The people who may ridicule you doubtless do not have the courage to enter into the creative domain or as many others have done, they have decided that they have no creative potential. They are wrong on both counts.

Nor is science a sacred cow. In fact, biologist-historian Dr. Everett I. Mendelson, of Harvard University stated, "Science, as we know it, has outlived its usefulness." The key to this quotation is the phrase "as we know it." There is no doubt that science has been the moving factor in building up our civilization—*as we know it*. But a reaction is setting in: the Age of Enlightenment of the eighteenth century, which extolled science as a reaction to the religious control that was determinative up to then, has run its course. More reflection is being done about the spirit, for it is said that science has atrophied the soul. One manifestation of a return to the spirit of man is the increasing interest in the unconscious as a fountainhead of values. Pascal's words ring true even today: "The heart has its own reasons for which reason itself has no answer."

There is ample evidence that by its very nature science is antithetical to creativity.

There are legions of examples where science, institutionally, arose against truly creative concepts offered to explain phenomena of which we know little. We have *established* explanations. We have enobled them by the word *fact*—but there are few facts, mostly beliefs and information handed down.

The latest example of the hostility of science to propositions or explanations that are different in kind than those heretofore accepted is that of Dr. Immanuel Velikovsky, Renaissance man extraordinary—paleontologist, archeologist, historian, physician, psychiatrist—offered an explanation for many natural phenomena. He was reviled by the scientific establishment. His publishers (Macmillan), who were going to bring out his book *Worlds in Collision*, were threatened by academics that if that book was published, Macmillan need not expect any of its publications to be used as classroom texts.

In fact, Harlow Shapley, prominent Harvard astronomer, who spearheaded the antagonism, is said to have plainly stated: "If Velikovsky is right then we are all damned fools."

Eventually, Velikovsky was vindicated on most counts in this book, though the establishment did not accept his ideas. And this did not take place because the scientific establishment became open-minded, but because the space probes sent aloft by NASA (National Aeronautics and Space Administration) brought back evidence that Velikovsky was right.

You may be apprehensive about departing from the party line of logic, and you may pride yourself on your logical mind. To do otherwise, you may feel, does not make sense.

But try the uncommon use of common sense. If you follow the logical pattern to solve your problem it does not necessarily lead to a creatively constructive solution. Remember, it is entirely likely that the logical approach, the common pattern, may not at all apply. And the application of a creative idea is not hard, as long as you get out of the accustomed way of doing—and into the intuitive. In fact, most creative ideas are deceptively simple.

For example, it is said that the popularity and availability of Coca-Cola was exponentially increased by a simple idea. A man approached the company and told them how they could do it—increase its use immensely—by bottling it for the mass market rather than selling it only as syrup to druggists.

Another simple idea concerns the use of nitroglycerine, long used in relieving anginal pain, a heart disease. Taken in the form of tablets put under the tongue, it works rapidly and most effectively.

Another recently successful mode of use of nitroglycerine is by external application. It arose by converting a detriment into an asset, as it was noted for decades that workers in factories making explosives often developed headaches from excessive exposure to nitroglycerine. This means nitroglycerine can be active when absorbed through the skin. This observation led to the making of a nitroglycerine ointment, which in a controlled dose, is absorbed through the skin for a longer-lasting effect when needed in the treatment of angina pectoris. (See Chapter 13, "Right Brain—Left Brain"; Chapter 15, "The Conscious and the Unconscious"; and Chapter 25, "Science and Insight.")

CHAPTER 9

Don't Institutionalize It Or You'll Kill It

A man can be a walking encyclopedia, extremely *clever*, but may lack wisdom as well as maturity. The symbol of the eternal student is well known: the individual who continues in school, continually taking course after course, filling himself with erudition. The reminder that I am raising here is that erudition is commonly equated with intelligence as well as with creativity, but it is related in only one facet. A creative person can use knowledge as a jumping-off-point into a creative endeavor, usefully, enriching others as well as himself—it is the daring—to see new relationships, new meanings to old symbols, linking familiar subjects to get new insights. And that is not the scenario of the eternal student.

Among the reasons that education or erudition with their rigidity and repetition do not equate with creativity is that schools must teach conformity, acceptance of "facts." They do not and cannot encourage insight because of the need to teach by repetition and drill, which distorts spontaneity, self-reliance, insight, discovery, intuition, insight, symbolic relationships. Hence, the longer the process of education (which is education of the mind not of the spirit), the longer the emotional adolescence, the more delayed the maturity. Direct living brings maturity—from action on the firing line, feedback and interaction between learning and making mistakes but then assessing them.

Yet the sort of mass education we have is necessary in a

mass society, though it is not directly conducive to self-knowledge, which is a lead into maturity.

What can be done in the light of the needs and demands of mass education in a mass society? There are no easy answers, and no single answer is known, as far as I am aware. The conflict begins in grade school between the teaching hierarchy and the child. It is hardened as the long educational process continues, and in modern society, more and more "facts" must necessarily be packed into the students.

But while society cannot seem to find an alternative for this suppression of creativity, the individual can help himself in various measures. First, if his *divine discontent* has precipitated him into questioning himself as to his role, he has become aware of a need. That is the first step.

Second, he should expand his horizon—various ways are discussed throughout this book.

Third, he should reassess his values. It may well be that in doing so he will decide that he is well satisfied with his state—materially, intellectually, emotionally—in which event he need look no further for he has come into his *summum bonum*, the supreme good. If he reassesses his values and is honest with himself in doing so, he should try again. It is more difficult to be honest with oneself, about oneself, than to be honest with others. Having reassessed his values and made what changes he deems important, he is probably ready to sail the thinly charted seas of creativity. How? By exposing himself to new experiences—reading, viewing, and other "how-to" experiences mentioned elsewhere in this book.

Fourth, the thrust of this chapter is, *Don't institutionalize it or you'll kill it*. In your attempt to forage in the forest of creativity, the temptation is to codify, to make an outline of *how-to-be-creative*. Don't! When you codify you kill it. There are a number of books by otherwise fine educators that do just that. They attempt to analyze and then synthesize, but the result is wooden or even deadening.

Creativity draws from a different fountain, marches to a different drummer. In fact, what it actually draws is sustenance largely from a part of the brain: the right hemisphere.

The brain is divided into two parallel-placed lobes or hemispheres connected by a cable or network of nerves. The left part of the brain controls the analytical, factual, logical, and mental functions, which are used in our daily endeavor. Most scientists, accountants, lawyers, architects, and those in similar occupations are largely *left-brain people*. Painters, musicians, writers, and other artists are largely *right-brain people* because creative capacities that people have or develop originate in the right hemisphere. It is also the hemisphere of feeling and intuition, and by the wonderful though unknown chemistry of the soul, moves people to soar in the creative activities.

When we *learn* something, the left hemisphere comes largely (though not exclusively) into play. The right hemisphere is concerned with the intuitive.

This is exactly the reason why when you institutionalize or codify attempts at creativity you are favoring the wrong instrument—the left brain. The educators who have written studies on creativity explain, hypothesize, and probably elucidate what we know of creativity, but they are using didactic and analytical as well as descriptive methods. They make you think, not feel. And feeling is visceral, not cerebral.

And, as previously discussed, you shift into a different category in a creative endeavor. It is not thinking in the common sense of the word, but feeling that has to be awakened. Intuition—then insight—arise from those areas. Hopefully, the use of intuition, leading to insight, both of which speak in the creative realm, lead to wisdom. Perhaps to maturity.

Logic is of the mind, irreplaceable in the areas that require a rigid, nondeviating instrument. Creativity is of the soul. (*See* Chapter 13, "Right Brain—Left Brain" and Appendix, and "Poetry and Creativity".)

CHAPTER 10

Instinct

Another quality, *instinct*, which is closely allied to intuition (or may virtually be the same in many contexts), has an important role in creativity. When you hear the expression, "My instinct told me," you will recognize that it arises from or has to do with the uncharted area of the soul or spirit. Frequently when faced with making a decision in which logic directs one course of conduct and instinct another, people will suppress their instinct and often fall flat on their faces. They do not trust their instincts. Actually instinct is often a dirty word among the rigid, logic-oriented people. They do not trust their instincts, they have divorced themselves from the spirit.

I must confess that having a scientific background and having bought the party line called "scientific method," which certainly is an important method in most aspects of science—except the creative—I have done just that for years. I suppressed or ignored the intuitive and followed the logical approach. Each time I suppressed the intuitive, I fell flat on my face.

One may be ignorant, but one need not be stupid. When faced with making a decision (and I usually make decisions quickly), when I have a clear or strong intuitive feeling about a direction or a given decision, I heed it, even though logic may dictate the opposite decision. And I have never regretted it.

There is an interesting example on the use of instinct by a writer who followed his instinct against all good advice to the contrary. E. B. White wrote a story that came to him in a dream. Eventually he developed a sympathetic children's story, celebrating *Stuart Little*, the child with the face of a mouse. An excellent publishing house accepted it.

In the course of production of the book, as is common, proofs were sent for comment to an individual knowledgeable in the world of books. That individual was a children's librarian, retired from the New York Public Library, who did free-lance work for publishers.

Upon reading the proofs she sent an earnest letter to the author urging him to withdraw the book because she did not like the book, the character, thought it was unfit for children, and warned him that it would harm his reputation.

But White followed his instincts, ignored the librarian's entreaty, and allowed the book to be published in the usual course of events.

Upon publication, the book was praised by reviewers and was quickly received by the reading public. In fact, even twenty years later, White continues to receive letters of appreciation from adult and child readers.

It was previously pointed out that children are basically creative. They have a better feel about separating fact from fancy than many adults—especially literal-minded retired librarians. White concludes that the fence between the real and fanciful is easily scaled by a child but seems to be an insurmountable obstacle to some adults. Adults, naturally, have had a longer time in which to become mentally rigid.

Don't forget: "And a little child shall lead them."

Yet a reasonable question may arise in the mind of those who wish to plug into creativity. How practical is it to dream, to feel? It all depends on what you are searching for. (Naturally, if, for example you are working in a control tower monitoring the flight of airplanes it would be fatal to dream.)

If you are looking for a *thing,* it is not practical because creativity will not produce it. But if you are searching in the land of concepts, ideas (which can often be translated into material goodies)—that is the realm of creativity. It is an antidote to boredom, provided that you invest yourself. Commitment or even passionate devotion is necessary in most areas, including interpersonal relations, to reap the fruits of an undertaking. Lukewarm interest produces lukewarm rewards.

In summary: Generally, there are four stages in which creativity operates:

1. Preparation: You must know something about the subject, though you need not be an expert, in which you invest your creative potential. This is a conscious stage. This is the stage that is a seeding of the loam of the creative soul; the individual reads, collects, accumulates raw material, may think of it intensely, or only allow the material to be absorbed without intensive efforts. *Chance favors the prepared mind*.

2. Incubation: The stage of incubation being preconscious or unconscious is intimately related to the creative act. During this stage consciousness is released, though the mind may not even be actively concerned with a problem. The individual may be relaxing or involved in other activities or his attention may be actively conscious in other directions. But during the stage of incubation a reshuffling or realignment occurs, spawning the creative combination. It may well be two old ideas in a new setting. Don't force it—don't try too hard.

3. Illumination: This is the peak reaction, the eureka, the oceanic feeling in which the solution suddenly, unexpectedly, and fully hits the individual in his act of creation. It is usually the full and complete answer to a problem or a puzzle, filling him with immense euphoria. He recognizes it immediately. And the creative individual may not even be aware that he has passed through the stages of preparation and incubation.

4. Verification: Some consider this an unnecessary state, for the full answer has hit at the moment of illumination. This is a stage where the goodness of fit of the product of illumination or of creativeness can be tested. It is predominantly necessary in science. In other areas, the product of illumination speaks for itself.

Part Two

This part of the book contains additional facets on creativity. There is here as well, a greater discussion of some of the topics covered in Part One of this book. From the detailed summaries on some of the aspects of creativity you will learn how to recognize your own creativity—what favors it and what holds it back.

CHAPTER 11

Creativity in Business

Do you want to know why the doings of your boss often drive you up the wall—how such a numbskull became boss? Perhaps, in this chapter, you will recognize some acts of your boss that drive you crazy—and you will understand. You may be able to help yourself—and help him—understand. It may even relieve some of your own anxiety on the job.

Were it not for creativity, business would be static. The average businessman prizes creativity, but mostly as a word. Commonly, he fears it because he does not understand it. The usual impression in business is that creativity is some quality artists and writers have to enable them to paint pictures or write.

Moreover, change is anathema to many business people—as well as to many other people. Change suggests something new, and the new is most often feared. When it is new *in kind*—such as creativity—there is a double resistance.

JUST BECAUSE IT IS NEW

People are often opposed to the new on principle. This is one of the reasons a businessman uses when he turns down a proposal—*it has not been proved.* (Obviously, if it has been proved it is not new—even by definition.) Another reason he may use to turn it down is that he does not feel that he can afford to be wrong. These two conditions alone are antagonistic to creativity and are conducive to stagnation.

Opposition to something new, at times mindless, is illustrated clearly by the early hostility of many to the automobile. Farmers would shallowly bury saws in the road—teeth up—so that an auto going over them would have its tires shredded.

Kettering, the genius of General Motors, held, "If you propose anything new I will give you a written guarantee on exactly what will happen: We present a thing and we know what they will do—they throw it in the wastebasket."

MINDLESSNESS

We have many contemporary examples of mindlessness. For example, a woman of seventy-one was sent to a hospital in a large medical center, which she reached by air, coming from her home in the Midwest, 1,500 miles away. She was admitted under Medicare. Months later, her family received a huge bill because Medicare had refused to pay the hospital, claiming the woman's admission to the hospital was "not medically necessary." The family objected, and they returned the bill with the explanation that *the patient died* in the hospital. Five months later, Medicare returned the bill stating again that payment would not be made because the admission to the hospital was "not medically necessary."

Because it often ignores the need for creativity, business or government hamstrings itself with other types of mindless operations—they need not be as outrageous as finding that a hospital admission was "not medically necessary" even though the patient died.

COMMUNICATION

One of the ways business suppresses creativity is by its failure in communication. What is the content of the communication that it ignores? Feedback. Acknowledgment. Follow-up. For example, giving an employee comment on his performance on the job. It does not matter how high or low the employee is on the hierarchical staff, but if the manager asks the employee to do something, then the manager should acknowledge that he is aware of performance by acknowledgment or feedback.

When you keep on accepting without acknowledging, you suppress an employee's spirit, or creativity, or even just his interest in his job. This is particularly true if an employee voluntarily gives an idea to the manager—whether it's about how to do a given operation better, a plan to get a new client, an idea for a new product, or whatever. It does not matter if the idea is not useful or practical. If the employee does not get feedback—not even being told that the idea was considered and not used—his interest in taking initiative in the future is reduced, or often crushed.

INDIVIDUALITY AND THE TEAM

The individual is often suppressed by another business practice: collectivism. We think of collectivism as applying to the Soviet system, as a socialistic word. But the *team approach* is a collective apparatus. And the team approach is inimical to individualism.

The reason individualism is important to consider is because creativity and individualism usually come in the same package; similar to creativity and nonconformity. Actually by definition, there is a conflict between individuality and conformity. It is not that the creative person is too lazy to conform or that he looks for trouble. But the fact is that conformity is group-think; and that suppresses the creative individual who thrives in the unstructured environment free of group pressure. Thus, an offensive against individuals is an offensive against creativity and eventually an offensive against the institution. The history of the world's civilization is witness to man's creativity.

Intrinsically, individuality is not easily digestible in an organization. In trying to digest a creative individual, an organization ill serves itself in that it suppresses what he could give to an organization. And it also serves the individual badly when it tries to subdue his free-flowing inventive spirit. Therefore this a plea for the individual, to allow him to use his creative faculties—not a plea against the organization. On the contrary, it is a plea to the organization not to follow a line of self-destructiveness.

The team approach to creativity has been tried and found severely wanting. It is called brain-storming, a type of group-think. There are no examples of which I am aware, where truly creative ideas or products have resulted from brain-storming. The team effort stimulates fellowship while in session—and destructive competition after it. William H. Whyte's *Organization Man* is also a plea to encourage an individual to utilize his creative ideas. Whyte makes an eloquent plea to business to allow itself to profit far better from the work of the creative individual by not forcing him into the slot of a team player. Thus everyone gains creatively.

Business, however, looks upon the group or team as a redemption of its ills. As a result, the organization settles down into the rut of nonthreatening mediocrity, which doesn't upset its unimaginative executives, while a creative person poses a real threat to them. The creative person, at times, may well strengthen the antagonism by his own thoughtless or undiplomatic behavior, which unfortunately emphasizes the animosity of the mediocre person against anyone whom he considers a "smart ass."

Thorstein Veblen (1857–1929), the American economist and sociologist who first came up with the term *conspicuous consumption*, was prescient in foreseeing the development of American managerial personnel into "trained incapacity." The Peter Principle is the second generation of trained incapacity. Moreover, other social and economic factors in our advanced industrial society also conspire to dampen the creative spark. Yet, there is no need for that to happen if an individual lives a thoughtful and creative life whether he be boss or employee.

HIRING PERSONNEL

Many thoughtful observers have called the recruitment of personnel a daily celebration of mediocrity. That is not amazing—antagonism snaps at the heels of every extraordinary person. He is extraordinary just by the fact alone that

he does not fit into the ready-made slots hewn out of mediocrity.

Would you hire Albert Einstein? On the basis of a survey
of employment applications eleven out of eighteen "top-
flight technical recruiters turned down an employment application with the name removed describing the education
and experience of Albert Einstein." Why? The reason given
was due to a lack of educational background.

But fourteen out of eighteen recruiters wanted to inter-
view another applicant (name removed) whose work was
described as having considerable experience in "design in
systems taking into account the role of the human being in
the use of machines to meet a functional objective." Who
was the nameless applicant? Rube Goldberg.

Who was the applicant whose application (name removed) was turned down by 100 percent of the top-flight
recruiters? It was the man who coined the term "cybernet-
ics" and who laid the groundwork for computer technology: Norbert Wiener.

The people chosen by the standard method of recruiters
on the basis of their standard criterion do have one talent
in common—they fit like an identical twin into the pattern
set forth in employment applications.

Business puts its own fate into the hands of personnel
recruiters, thereby making an absurd assumption *that personnel people can run its business*! Obviously illogical, but
that is how it works. Personnel picked by recruiters are
expected by business to run its business successfully. Has
business ever thought that the next logical step should be to
test the business acumen and business judgment of personnel recruiters whom business expects to have enough insight and judgment to pick applicants who can successfully
run a business?

Personnel screening is successful in keeping out people
who do not fit into a niche, a standard pattern. In other
words, this practice and pattern assures mediocrity. And
they may be partially right. Business goes on, though a
considerable percentage of firms fail. This is despite the
abundance of mediocrity that assiduously suppresses creativity in potentially valuable people. Business, in its pursuit

of the average, which fits its predetermined job slots, has never realized, or not taken into account, that a first-class mind cannot be replaced by several mediocre minds.

DECISIONS, DECISIONS

Business is a never-ending procedure of making decisions. It is often as much of a question of which old, well-known and tried remedy to apply to a problem, as it is which new approach to use in viewing the question or need on hand, and devising a method of handling it. That would be a *new* remedy. Creativity is necessary in both, though the application of an old remedy is not considered to be one fraught with hazards. But make a wrong decision even in selecting an old remedy, and you will reap failure, even though the remedy is tried and true.

But decisions made by the mediocre executive compared to those made by the creative one do usually differ. And the creative executive does not necessarily have to devise a great and ingenious method in solving a problem. Making the selection among old, previously tried methods often presents enough of a problem. But the basic difference between the commonplace and creative problem solver is this: The field of vision of the creative one is broader, he looks for a greater universe from which to choose his solution. Since the power centers of management are inimical, if not hostile, to the creative spirit, let us examine on what influences each of them bases a decision.

Criteria for Decision-making:

By Mediocre People	By Creative People
Surveys and data.	Hunches.
Team and consensus.	Individual ideas.
Precedent.	Innovation.
Standards and patterns.	Deviations from patterns.

Fear often a component.	Fear seldom a component.
Solution specialized—narrowed to the immediate problem.	Solution broad—can often be extrapolated into other areas.
Hard, documented approach.	Speculative approach.
Levels are tangible.	Levels may be tangible with abstract overtones.
Will depend on reports, recommendations and other data to exculpate the decision maker if decision is wrong one, as he fears to be wrong.	Will depend on his intuition and "feel" and does not avoid a solution that appears sound, though he may be wrong.
Uses convention as a framework—goes by the book.	Often rejects the conventional.
The objective is maintenance of status quo and criterion is largely material compensation.	Also seeks material compensation, but the psychological income is of preeminent importance—such as recognition.

What then is it that blunts creativity in a creative person—negativeness, criticism, and hostility. For a number of reasons these three responses, which somehow have come into a job and have not been filtered out by restrictive recruiting or personnel policies, are often used in business in its contact with its creative personnel.

Conversely, what stimulates the creative person and enhances the quality of sound decisions in business and elsewhere?

(1) Encouragement to express his ideas without fear of ridicule or hostility, even though he will often meet a nega-

tive decision. In fact, many creative people, as a result of their experience with management develop an almost paranoid trait and expect to see their ideas rejected.

Many creative people have told me that they believe negativeness by management is a knee-jerk reaction. Therefore, when practical, they offer the opposite of an idea that they want to promote. In an overwhelming proportion of occasions, management says "no." As a result, the creative person puts into action the opposite of their proposed idea, which was all along what he wanted to try. This should be a valuable mirror to management—it should look at the image of itself it creates. In my own experience in an appreciable number of instances the mirror reflects a true image.

(2) Permissiveness is an attitude as well as a response. Creative people thrive in a permissive atmosphere, which does not at all mean that a permissive attitude makes anarchy out of an organization. For example, management cannot accede to everything a creative person wants. To stimulate a permissive atmosphere try to say, "Yes, but . . ." when you necessarily have to turn down a request. This is reminiscent of the permissive lady who, when asked by her son if she had ice cubes, said "Yes, but they're not frozen."

(3) Reading, on a variety of subjects in areas other than your own specialties, expands one's horizon; then reflection may stimulate a creative ferment.

(4) Creative ideas come more readily in the time between sleeping and waking, the time when the censoring faculties of the cerebral centers of the brain are at their least efficient. Therefore your *zombie time*, when the restraining influence of "knowledge," i.e., the *common sense* of knowing that you cannot do this or that is the weakest, may well be your strongest creative time.

(5) In statistics a method called the *goodness of fit* is one of the tests applied to determine if the method that one proposes to apply to solve a problem fits—if it is consistent with a comparison of one's previous experience. Or, in other words, with what precedent does one wish to compare a proposed plan?

But the application of the rule of precedent is often unfortunate in creativity. It is said that the reason lawyers are not particularly noted for creativity is because their whole orientation is by precedent. When you look back for a pattern, your view will tend to freeze, and you may not be as open-minded in evaluating a new alternative. I know it's more comfortable to follow a pattern (and sometimes weaken and do it), but it does not give you the advantage of possible improvement.

Adherence to tradition, pattern, or precedent are all quite related in their detrimental influence on creativity. Another trait that is equally inimical to creativity is analysis—discussed under different topics in this book. Analysis, the process of tearing down, is the opposite of synthesis. It is looking at the parts and not the whole. Perhaps that is the reason engineers are not reputed to be particularly creative. In fact, schools of engineering have more recently attempted to open the training of engineers to include subjects or ideas that may stimulate a creative stance, outlook, and approach. The development of skills and knowledge of analysis is also needed in certain endeavors. But it produces a mental cast that feeds and regurgitates mathematical formulas, a feat requiring only memorization and rote learning, which are the death of creativity.

Nonetheless, creativeness can profitably be applied even in engineering. E. D. Dean, professor of engineering at the New Jersey Institute of Technology (formerly Newark College of Engineering), is one of the new breed of engineers who recognizes it and states, "The higher you go in business the more decisions are really made by intuition . . . and the top men apparently have it working for them." Samuel C. Florman's *The Existential Pleasure of Engineering* points out how the necessary mechanical thinking of engineering can be fructified by an open mind to the creative approach. Thus it is being slowly recognized in business that the *middle-of-the-road* person who makes no waves is in effect a *middle-of-the-rut* person.

CHAPTER 12

Business and Loyalty

Business has many catchwords or attitudes it sets out as beacons to guide its employees. Many can become meaningless and often laughable. One such is loyalty.

Children model their actions on what their parents *do* rather than what they ask their children to do. For example, many parents tell their children not to lie. How effective will that training be when children find that their parents lie joyously and frequently? Children cannot distinguish ordinary common lies from bleached lies, which is what the socially acceptable so-called white lies really are. They will ignore those parental injunctions not to lie. What is of more far-reaching importance, they will lose confidence in their parents when they find them lying—after having been told that "lying is bad."

Children also become disenchanted when they find their favorite hero on TV switching loyalties. For example, children urge their mothers to buy Zilch cereal because their favorite hero on TV extolls it. Then the Zilch cereal hero switches loyalties and appears on a new show that promotes Crackpot cereal. What is a child to believe? What is he to believe when his favorite baseball hero is traded and then plays just as enthusiastically on a competing team?

Similarly, management sets a model by its own behavior. In its house organs, pep talks, or veiled threats, business extolls the virtue of loyalty to the organization. But an executive of one company jumps to the next job and advancement—to a competitive company. Naturally, he would join a competitor for a job that is prized in industry. Business expects its employees to give loyalty. Is it loyal to its employees? Let us see how this stacks up.

The standards for an employee seem to be set in shifting sand. Added to the shock to an employee that loyalty is an illusion, a myth, there is a creeping insecurity: How safe is my own job?

There is no loyalty in business. There is also an erosion of loyalty in interpersonal relations. That is probably the result of situation ethics: What ethic shall I use under such-and-such given circumstances. What will best serve my interests? Perhaps this arises in the social matrix, and the absence of loyalty in business is merely a reflection of the alienating society. We have replaced our heroes with celebrities—dull, vacuous, plastic men and women whose personalites have been created by press agents.

What then should business do to retain some semblance of loyalty—that dependability that was called loyalty but which no longer exists? To tell employees to "work hard and you will be rewarded" is at best naive and at worst dishonest. Reward is not largesse, it is payment for services performed. Employees are not feudal subjects of the boss.

Buy an employee's loyalty? You cannot buy loyalty any more than you can buy love. The employee whose loyalty you can buy is open to the next bidder who comes along and raises the price of loyalty above that which has recently been bought.

To get dependability, perhaps another face of the trait often called loyalty, it is necessary to *fill the employee's psychological needs* even more than the financial.

How?

Respect his feelings—the mechanization of society mechanizes people. They react in a stereotyped or ritualized way. They don't act, they react. A manager often criticizes and sometimes insults the people responsible to him, even in the presence of coworkers. This may well serve the faltering ego of the manager (perhaps he is castrated by his wife when he gets home), but it hurts the functioning of business. When you need to take issue with an employee, don't fail to do so, but tell him kindly how he failed to perform the job. And be specific. The volume and tone of voice is as important—and can be more important—than the content of what is said. *How* you say something describes you more clearly than you would suspect.

But especially tell him whenever he performs his job well. Will he ask for a raise if you praise him? If he deserves a raise he should get it, it will redouble his efforts. It is usually cheaper to give a raise than to train a replacement.

Give support. Show it. Above all be straight with people.

By all means encourage creativity. The methods are outlined in this and other chapters of this book. You will fill the poverty in an employee's soul and spirit—those areas where too many of us are paupers. The stormy petrel, the disrupter of the sleepy organization, is often the most valuable person if you are taking a long-range view of the life and health of your organization. Thus the nonconformist, the individualist can be and often is, the *most loyal* member of an organization—if you still think in terms of the loyalty prevalent before job-hopping became the smart thing to do. By stimulating creativity in the creative member of your organization you are building two irreplaceable traits that are without price! Respect and affection on the part of the whole organization, though they may actually dislike the creative person because they are threatened by him.

Is feeding the creative person an unfailing remedy for organizational health? Emphatically no. Nor am I aware of any nonfailing remedy since overseers with whips were outlawed. They were effective—in building pyramids. Presumably you want to build a memorial but not a pyramid.

While most people have creative potential, only a very few are creative. What do you do with hopeless duds? If you are positive that they are hopeless and are sure they are blanks you can do nothing. In fact, many people do not want responsibility, do not want to rise, take risks, or dare. They are also necessary in an organization to fill slots that require only hands. Such jobs would drive most creative people mad, they would be worse at such jobs than duds. I do not know a remedy for such a situation. You cannot get loyalty—or a reasonably accurate facsimile thereof—if you reduce an employee's security. And his security can be easily threatened in a number of ways, especially when he puts himself in the place of a man who was summarily fired. *I may be next,* he may think—and he may well be right. If you have to fire someone, do so resolutely, but let the staff know why. Presumably, you have a good and persuasive reason. Otherwise, other employees may feel that the boss is merely exercising his privilege of whims and caprice. Loyalty or morale in an organization fall when you make a sharp and dishonest business deal—even with someone from the outside. People feel, *there, but for the grace of God am I.*

For example, the Bon Ami company some years ago announced that it would pay an advance and royalty to anyone who would suggest a way *that it would use,* in which the company could profit from. An individual from the outside proposed that the company raise the wholesale price of its products, two cents per gross. This would not disturb the retail price structure because dealers would not pass on to the consumer 1/72 of a cent, and it would bring more money into the company. The company used the idea but refused to pay the person who suggested it.

In court, this creative person unfortunately lost. The basis on which the judge ruled against him was that anyone could have thought of it. The fact that no one, and above all the company had not, is obvious. Judges are "experts," (I don't know in what) and thus a lack of judgment and unfairness can almost be expected to surface. This was hardly an event that raised good morale. The company gets away with what it can—why shouldn't I? Am I next for a rip off? Who knows?

A profile of a businessman: The businessman is often unjustly singled out for calumny. True, some businessmen are economic brigands, and were they not in a mercantile business they would be thugs. A rather mild obloquy is that the businessman is a robber baron. But with government control, growing like a cancer into an increasing number of areas, he cannot act like one for long.

Indeed, the businessman has his problems. The larger his enterprise grows, the more precipitous his ruin can be. And the bottom-line area between the black and the red—success and ruin—is not wide and often threateningly narrow. He is neither a coward nor a bully but can be both; he is neither a vulture nor a diplomat, though he is more often the former than the latter, in the name of competition.

The businessman has also been made a whipping boy in literature. Some books, as William Whyte's *Organization Man* castigate him with a considerable amount of justification. But others are also flailing out at him. Joseph Heller's *Something Happened* shows the reflection of his action in his personal life. In *Catch 22* Heller also attacked businessmen in the guise of the military, for as a fact, the military and business have much in common.

A trenchant study of the modern businessman will be found in Michael Maccoby's *The Gamesman,* which assesses various types of businessmen and their almost predictable traits. While he describes other types—*company men* who are the descendants of the organization man, *jungle fighters* who are the piranhas, killing for the sake of killing, even exceeding needs of the competitive acts—he gives the stage to the new breed, the *gamesman,* who arose in the 1970s. Not that he is an entirely new breed—his traits were preceded by other types; but the emphases make the difference. While the daring gamesman makes a show of concern for his employees—only in the interests of intelligent selfishness—he eviscerates his relations of any feelings. He is a dynamic man, a winner who is merciless with losers. He suppresses any involvements that are personal, and atrophies his feelings of love, warmth, and friendship. One of his bywords is that a man coming up cannot afford to have friends. Soon, his life motif becomes the injunction that one cannot afford to feel.

But singling out the businessman as a suppressor of creativity or as a scapegoat for economic or social ills is missing the point by a wide margin. That is because one fails to see him in a larger scope—his role in *business as an institution.*

Call him businessman and you may fail to see the institutional texture of his make-up at work and how his actions and reactions are a component of an institution. Whether it is a mercantile establishment, the military, an ecclesiastical setting, a nonprofit foundation, (frequently of no profit to anyone) or even the political business of government—the institutional and bureaucratic nature and purpose of each is intrinsically similar. The methods may look different and the hypocrisies may have different colors or directions, but the differences between the expressed aims and the true aims inherent among various institutions are quite similar. In none of them are the expressed aims the same as the true aims.

Institutions tend to depersonalize in various degrees, depending on the nature of the institution. Perhaps the process of depersonalization is essentially greatest in the military as an institution; perhaps the least in a mercantile institution, and as a rule, the smaller the business the less the depersonalization.

The businessman—manager, administrator, supervisor, boss—also suffers some of the depersonalization. One of the great dangers besetting him as an individual is when he brings his business or occupational persona into his personal life. It is like a lawyer who brings his rhetoric home, and who handles his familial relationships with his wife or his children like a prosecuting attorney or as an advocate. In either case it smacks of hypocrisy, and that is clearly sensed by the family member who is on the receiving end, whether he is the object of the lawyer's attacking persona (prosecutor) or the recipient of his role as defender (the advocate part). In either event the familial interaction is unhealthy, with unsatisfying results to everyone concerned.

Similarly, the businessman who brings his business mentality or rhetoric home is riding for a fall in his interpersonal, familial relationships. So are members of the family, though the likelihood is that the family unit will stay together because the material goodies supplied by the father-businessman may provide manna to his wife, as well as to his children going to college.

But what about the businessman himself? Business conduct is by and large soulless, and its attitude brought into the family context gives little sustenance to the soul, the spirit of the family members, or to him. And some members, including the businessman, miss that spice of life.

In order to enhance the fleeting spice of life, one or both spouses attempt to augment that flavor by steps that divide rather than unify the family. The wife may take a lover, the husband a mistress. Fine, if the marital problem is solved. But usually it is intensified because each magnifies his own dissatisfactions, blaming the spouse for his or her own actions to reduce accompanying feelings of guilt. "See what you made me do?"

Other unsought-for events dilute the interpersonal cement: relative sexual impotence on the part of the successful businessman, or other disturbances of sexual function such as premature ejaculation. *When a marriage is on the rocks, the rocks are in the bed.* You have no doubt often noted that the man who is a firebrand at the office often has a dragon at home.

Is creativity a remedy against impotence? Not at all. But creativity can put an individual together emotionally. It can be a safe and effective remedy against two modern diseases—boredom and depression (without side effects) and against the ennui of life. Life may be full of material goodies, but the vessel remains empty. Creativity may well supply a remedy because it is fulfilling, not depleting, to the soul.

Businessmen and others may find that some of the effects of creativity will supply the joy of creation, which is almost orgasmic. But he may never have thought of it as an activity or accoutrement of a respectable person. Golf, yes—gardening, yes—sailing, yes. These are respectable and not way-out as are some of the activities of creative people. But these so-called respectable activities are narcissistically inclined toward your doing something primarily for yourself alone.

What's wrong with that? Nothing, if you feel content, not disaffected, or only occasionally have a horrifying feeling of utter emptiness in a matrix of profound loneliness.

But if you feel that your internal milieu can be improved, try to invest yourself in something *outside of your-*

self. This is the area in which creativity flourishes. And I don't mean to suggest do-gooder activities. You may have potential gifts that you have never explored. If you explore them you may find a new world.

Again, the thing is to get involved *outside of yourself.*

A businessman is accustomed to look at a situation in the light of "What will it do for me." That is splendid. Creativity may well do something, or a lot, for you. But look further than the immediate. In business often there develops an attitude where people are looked at with the implicit thought, "I'll be nice to him because he can be useful to me." Try the simple *I'll-be-nice-to-him* formula. The dividends can be larger, but the coin will be different.

Above all, don't fear to take a heretofore unaccustomed step. Remove self-censorship—censorship of your act.

But you will have to take unaccustomed steps. Many of them will not conform to the criteria of being *practical,* according to your customary criteria.

Consider one businessman who was highly successful in his business but who began to doubt how successful he was as a person. He told me how he took his first steps with creativity. He began to observe, and to give an unimportant item a second thought.

He had on his desk a finger moistener that he used to dampen his finger when he was turning the numerous pages of reports that he was reading. When the moistener was dry it was refilled with water. But whenever it was refilled, his secretary would tell him (and he often saw it himself) that mold or slime had formed on the bottom. It was cleaned out before refilling (when his secretary was not disgusted at getting rid of the slime.) But even when refilled and clean, the thought occurred to him that he was always moistening his fingers with slime. Often they bought a new moistener, but the same thing happened with one use—slime formed on the bottom.

It was not a crucial matter, it was merely disgusting to him. That moved him to try to do something. He had a bright idea; why not refill the moistener with Listerine instead of water? He did. It worked. No more slime.

That small step gave him considerable satisfaction, especially as he was ready to take his first step into creativity. It was a perfect opportunity, and he told me that it gave him more satisfaction than if he had received a large order that netted him a bonus.

With that small encouragement, and nothing is really petty because it may be the doorway to a new area, he became more observant. And aware. One day he wanted a small shelf built above the sink in the bathroom next to his office to hold soap, which became messy when put on the side of the sink. Instead of sending out for brackets and wood, he thought to himself: What is the common denominator that brackets may have with other objects around the office? Simple, a right angle with two flat surfaces. Ah, his glance fell on book ends. The bottom of a book end—the side that sits flat on the shelf—can be put against the wall. The other side, which holds up books, will protrude. Putting up two book ends against the wall with tacks gave him a surface on which to put a narrow piece of cardboard, making a shelf.

Subsequently he told me that these two experiences enabled him not only to develop truly creative ideas in marketing, which was his business, but also they gave him an entirely new dimension in his personal life.

Nothing is too petty—it may well work for you.

Other executives told me how they intensified their own creativity. One man became cognizant that other people might not infer what he implied in his impersonal business letters and decided to give them some life. What he did was this:

Quite often he did not sign his letters, his secretary affixed his name with the customary small initials that secretaries use to indicate that they have signed for the boss. Becoming more aware of things outside of himself—in this instance, people—he realized that the recipient of a letter may well feel that he is not important enough, a letter to him is signed by a functionary. The executive still didn't want to spend time signing every letter, even when he was in the office. But he remedied their impersonal nature by having his secretary add a sentence after she affixed his name: "Signed in Mr. Smith's absence by EBR."

Innovation needs an open mind. But before an open mind can function it must be an observant one. It is truly said that it is not computers but closed-minded executives who crush creativity.

Strategy is necessary in business. While the word strategy has a military origin, in modern usage it connotes a plan, an approach toward the solution of a problem. And plans are necessary in human endeavors to anticipate, to find alternative paths toward an objective, in short, the purpose of *strategies*.

Strategies are creative acts. A businessman who may think creativity is not in his métier has unknowingly used it when planning his sales and other strategies.

Creativity is perhaps at its height when a compelling need exists, it may mean survival. When Rome was growing, not only enlarging its territory but wanting to retain the territories it had won, creativity was at its height in various strata of Roman society.

One well-known stratagem was used by Hannibal, the Carthaginian general of the second century B.C., to rout the enemy. He tied burning torches to the tails of elephants who then ran amok among the enemy's soldiers. Another stratagem was used by the Allies in World War II in the conquest of Africa from Rommel's forces. Salt water was diverted into the pipes that carried water to the enemy. The disorganization of the German army followed soon after.

A businessman using strategy in his business is limited by only three factors: first his ethics; second, the law; third, his creativity. Unfortunately, strategy is a fact of life in various jungles.

A businessman will further develop his creativity by accepting risks with the challenges, even risks to his ego. He will not fear to be wrong. He will encourage the creativity of others and in that way will enrich his own milieu. He will define his goals broadly. For example, he will not ask how he can improve his pension plans to prevent his employees' changing jobs but rather how to maximize job continuity. This is similar to the classical situation that says, don't ask how to build a better mousetrap, ask how to catch mice more efficiently. In that way your mind will not be limited to mouse traps.

A creative person will not fear to take an 180° turn—he may learn something thereby. For example, advertising says that you must get the consumer to identify with the product. While speaking that party line, advertising people forget it in deed.

For example, there is strong agitation against the use of cigarettes. Cancer societies and other institutions are running public service advertisements showing a black lung as the result of smoking. The instillation of fear has been a successful stratagem to induce people to use certain products, as underarm deodorants. They *fear to offend.* They want to identify with a person who doesn't have body odor. *But people don't identify with lungs*—black or otherwise. And cigarette consumption is continually increasing.

A successful campaign against cigarettes may well be one in which a cigarette smoker is being ridiculed. Show a scene—a dinner party or other gathering—in which the person smoking is being laughed at by the other, nonsmoking, people. A smoker will readily identify with another smoker who is a whole person, not a disembodied lung. Put that person into an idiotic stance, and the cigarette smoker identifying with another prominently pictured smoker will see himself in an asinine situation. His self-esteem will be reduced. All people want the esteem, respect, affection if not love, of their peers. Fragile egos need support. Very few people have enough self-esteem and self-acceptance— guts—to expose themselves to the ridicule of others and continue acts that make them objects of ridicule. No one aspires to be a clown.

As long ago as the third century B.C., Aristotle observed that man is a political animal. This applies to all areas of man's activities, and more particularly in business. The employee, no matter how high in the hierarchy, tries to please the current climate. Except sometimes he cannot.

Fortunately, the tremendous influence for good that creativity represents is beginning to be recognized by business, though with mincing steps. A recent event may be interpreted that it is growing in acceptance. In October

BUSINESS AND LOYALTY   103

1976 William S. Paley, chairman of the CBS empire, suddenly fired Arthur R. Taylor, the president of CBS, with the statement that Taylor did not show "flair" in his management. Flair? Taylor had just finished off a most successful year—in income. Apparently, that was not enough. Flair, creativity is what was wanted. Perhaps we can believe Paley, though man being a political animal, he probably had more compelling reasons than "flair." (See Appendix "What are We Living For?")

CHAPTER 13

Right-Brain—Left-Brain
in Creativity

In previous chapters it was stated that creativity is a compound of many traits—that creative people have, use, or develop certain faculties that are associated with creativity. Where do they arise? What makes these people tick, or not tick? How can one elicit these traits, nurture them to grow into luxuriance?

Our brain is composed of two halves or hemispheres. Imagine these two hemispheres to be two footballs, standing upright side by side, with the ends of each football pointing up and down. Then imagine a rope or heavy string connecting them.

That is an oversimplified model of how the two hemispheres of the brain are attached to each other. The rope connecting them is called the *corpus callosum*, which is a cable of nerves allowing intercommunication between both hemispheres. It is through this cable that sensations felt or impressions gained are sent to the brain and are synthesized and interpreted into judgment and action. The right brain knows what the left one is doing, and *vice versa*.

But each hemisphere has a different predilection, each virtually handles different activities, responds to different signals, and sends out different kinds of impulses. They have their own particular form of mind activity or intellect. The right brain is the hemisphere that has traits that predominately characterize the creative or the intuitive individual; the left brain is the hemisphere that deals predominantly with the factual and analytical aspects of man's thinking. Thus, creativeness is predominantly a right hemisphere phenomenon. The accountant's, lawyer's, or engineer's activity is that predominantly of the left hemisphere.

Here are some comparisons of the functions or traits of right-hemisphere- and left-hemisphere-oriented people:

Right-hemisphere People	Left-hemisphere People
These usually do not understand a balance sheet.	These, as accountants, usually are poor in product design, or other development.
They go into a task by doing it, act on a "hunch" or an intuitive feel.	They will not go into a task unless they first develop a chart with its planning in detail, ignore hunches.
Have a strong emotional component in their actions or decisions.	The principal component in their actions or decisions is intellectual.
Their thinking is holistic.	Their thinking is specialized, linear, logical, thing-oriented, almost literal.
Will enter a project despite chaos.	Will enter only in an orderly fashion, following a plan or go by the book.
Will do a number of tasks simultaneously.	Act sequentially, or consecutively, one thing at a time.
See relationships rather than hard-and-fast "facts."	Relationships are based on hard-and-fast "facts."
Are implicit in their relationships with people.	Demand explicit relationships only.

Are sensitive to modulation of voice, gesturing, body language.	Depend on what is said. They ignore the nonverbal signals.
Experimental.	Tried and true; worship the sure thing.
Speculative.	Logical.
See a gestalt, are holistic.	Only analytical, well articulated, tit-for-tat.
Can manage people.	Better in management planning.
Theme is synthesis.	Theme is analysis.
Act on intuition.	Act on analysis.
Reflection and action.	Action on a survey or report.
Visual-imaginative.	Nonvisual.
Will daydream—have deep imaginative involvement.	Work hard and play hard— flat on emotional involvement.
Work on a level above the rational.	Work on a rational level only.
Cannot be simulated by computer.	Can be simulated by computer.
Educational system decries these qualities.	Aim of educational system is to strengthen these qualities.
Frequently communicate nonverbally.	Always communicate verbally.
Creative.	Implementive.

Do not misunderstand and think that right-brain people are the salt of the earth and left-brain people are rejects. *That is not true.* We need both kinds of thinking in the functioning of our society, in fact almost any society needs the dreamers, and inventors, and those with courage to make glorious fools of themselves. But it just as acutely needs those who implement, and even act as a brake occasionally. You wouldn't have a right-brain person keep the books of a company any more than you would ask left-brain people to make inductive leaps or develop decisions where people's reactions are involved. As a matter of fact in business and other institutions, there is an irreplaceable need for left-brain policy planners and as much of a need for right-brain advisors who make inductive leaps into the future. The left-brain person, going by the book, needs evidence, charts, and systems—by then, it may be too late to act. The right-brain person makes the best and most effective leader because he is plugged in on the unconscious, provided that he has the linear trait of left-brain people, the ability to articulate and convey an idea.

One may well ask if one is inclined to developing right-brain characteristics, how does the right-brain predominance originate?

Many investigators in the right-brain—left-brain domain believe that the predominance of one or the other is genetically determined. No one really knows. But take heart if you don't know whether genetically you are a right-brain person. Even if you are, you can suppress it—mass education necessarily suppresses it if only to keep the student body manageable. And then uninspiring as well as noncreative teachers finish the job.

But assuming you are a left-brain person and you want to adapt some creative traits. The world is open to you. First, trust yourself. If you have a feel or hunch—don't suppress it. Let it come out. You may be right. And most important, the subjective experience you will have will become cumulative. And with practice it will become easier and more natural to you. That in itself will make you more adept in the creative area.

Here are more suggestions on enhancing right-brain

function. Don't just read how to do it—do it. Listen to your inner self. Act on a hunch, especially if you have not done so customarily (obviously, don't jump into an irrevocable situation on every impulse). Have confidence that you will get a spark and you will. Be open to new experiences in feeling as well as thinking. Daydream by all means, but naturally (if for example you are a controller in an airport tower monitoring the movement of airpanes you don't just daydream). Read some Persian poetry such as Hafiz and Firdusi, and let the feelings and sensations get to you.

Above all learn to *meditate*. Transcendental meditation or the relaxation response will open up new areas.

CHAPTER 14

Getting Acquainted with Your Emotions

In the preceding chapter we discussed the phenomenon of the left and right hemispheres of the brain and suggested that the right one perhaps holds the trigger to emotions. And emotions are the vehicles through which creativity expresses itself, or through which creativity is sparked.

If emotion is profoundly involved in creativity, and the right-brain has strong emotional connotation, we ought to look at emotions—briefly, clearly, and open-mindedly.

Emotions arise in the area of feeling. (In the literature you will come across the word "affects"—it has to do with feelings, such as love, hate, envy, joy, etc.)

Apparently there is something deeper to the left- and right-hemisphere phenomenon. You are familiar with people who have color blindness, where certain colors, more particularly, red and green, or blue and yellow appear gray to their eyes. There are also people who have *feeling blindness*. Their ideation and responses are gray, colorless. They can talk intelligently and logically. They may be, and usually are, fine conversationalists. But their conversation is about *things*, or about actions or events, or even about other people. But the *content* of their conversation is virtually free from emotion. They say nothing of how they feel about actions, or events or people about whom they are talking.

These people know emotive words such as angry, joyous, etc., but they cannot really tell how it feels to be angry or joyous or what happens to you in the gut when you are angry or joyous. They can show rage occasionally but cannot tell you how it feels to be enraged, or outraged. It is not because they lack words. They merely lack feelings. Their speech is factual or colorless, no modulation in voice, no body language or gestures. Successful businessmen and many other people are conditioned by their subculture or calling to show no emotion. They have adopted early the ability to mask, then repress their feelings, and it makes up their persona.

Do they have fantasies? Perish the thought! Fantasies have an emotional coloring. These emotion-blind people rarely project themselves outside of their self-centered universe, which is constructed to be safe from any emotional invasion. They are middle-of-the-road people and feel safe in the middle of their rut.

It follows that they are wooden, rather than creative people. Creativity presupposes getting out of the self-centered universe, exposing oneself to sensations and emotional influences, and taking risks.

This is an example of distinctly left-brain people. While most people are *predominantly* one or the other, such people are distinctly left brain. They may well be highly successful in their business—if money is their ultimate picture of success. Less driving people may have file-clerk mentalities with hardly a spark in their spirit.

An example of the latter is a lady who is director of publicity in a large and respected publishing house. The publicity department sends out new books to magazines, newspapers, journals, and such periodical publications for review. Book reviews are read by the general public, which usually and unfortunately buys books based on reviews. Every publisher, through its publicity department, cultivates reviewers in order to encourage them simply to review its books since it usually cannot manipulate reviewers to review its books favorably.

A scientist of my acquaintance is also book review editor of a scientific journal. But he does not limit the reviews he writes to scientific books, after all, he reasons, some scientists also think like people—after hours. So he also reviews worthwhile books on the human condition, on the current scene, or those which have a philosophical cast.

Noting that a particular book had recently been published on the influence that political polls have on the voting decisions of people, he felt the book might be worth reviewing in his scientific journal. After all, some scientists also vote. Hence, he personally telephoned the publicity director and asked for a review copy for his journal. (He had previously received from that publisher only scientific books for review.)

The publicity director could not understand why a scientific publication would review a book that did not deal in science, and she refused the request. (It should be remembered that her job is to get *all the reviews she can!*)

Was this an example of a creative person? On the contrary, her action is an example of the least intelligent stratum of a clerk mentality with no spark of even average understanding. She reacted like Pavlov's dog (bell rings—saliva; no bell rings—no saliva; science journal—scientific book; science journal—nonscience book—bang, no good). This is an excellent example of obliviousness—the publicity director was being oblivious to the purpose of her job.

Another person, such as the successful executive or professional man who has feeling blindness and avoids emotion, may indirectly come upon emotional problems. He has success, recognition, money, position, hence power and the prestige. He gained them by competition, being more adroit than other people with whom he was competing. Then, *competition per se becomes the end-objective* with him. He will lose sight of the fact that the role of competition is merely the means toward his rise in the values he holds dear. *The means become the end.* Hence, anything that puts him in a lower stratum is viewed as a personal failure and takes its toll on him. In his catechism, failure is worse than treason or murder.

The failure can be a negligible event—not scoring better than anyone at golf (golf is the ritual of business contact). But failure is the opposite of success in his catalogue of values. It does not matter how petty the failure, it is deeply anxiety-producing to the man with a success syndrome.

As the result of such failures the man breaks. How? At the time when he is at his pinnacle of success he reasons that he cannot afford a failure. And one failure produces another. His powerful exterior values push him in his fifties as inexorably as they did in his twenties or thirties. But he suddenly cannot eat garlic, his digestive system is normally more sluggish in his fifties, though he can now certainly afford the most luxurious French fare. Failure again. His neuromuscular apparatus is in excellent shape, but not that of a man in his twenties, and therefore the stress takes its toll in strength and coordination—failure on the golf course. Stomach ulcers are not the ultimate failure because our culture decrees it is a badge of honor, the sign of a successful though empty executive. But fatigue created by tension and anxiety is disturbing to him. Performance is his goal. The last straw about performance that lays him into the mire of anxiety and illness, psychological and often physical, is sex.

He cannot perform as he used to—in other words, in business he surpassed his last year's quota, but in his sexual life he is going in the other direction. The first time he cannot get an erection or has premature ejaculation he is sure that he has personally failed.

But he is a doer, a success-oriented man. How can he personally fail? He has to fix it *himself*. Hasn't he always fixed problems in business—most successfully? His remedy is oblivion—alcohol. Drink will make the problem go away. But naturally with alcohol it gets worse. With drinking, sex naturally and expectedly dips low—alcohol is a depressant to the nervous system.

Impotence is often a psychic matter as well as physical. But after all, he reasons, he's not crazy—he wouldn't think of going to a shrink. Psychotherapy is for kooks, the crazies. Hasn't his wife gone to one for years now—and she isn't a better wife.

Obviously, psychotherapy to help him to be honest with himself would be a step in the right direction. Or even counseling, namely discussion regarding his values, such as they are, would be splendid. But when a business problem occurs, no successful executive looks for help from others except that he delegates work to lower echelons, otherwise he handles it himself. To look for help in the emotional area would be, to him, an abysmal failure as a person.

He has lost all semblance as an individual. He is a corporate animal. The somewhat-less-than-human executive has now been totally dehumanized—virtually depersonalized.

The problem is deeper than a psychological one—it is also philosophical and sociological. Our materialistic culture further dehumanizes many a man who is essentially empty emotionally. It is this emptiness that enabled him to rise. But now, when it comes in events that really matter to the individual, he has fallen.

Creativity per se is not the royal remedy—good for what ails you. Creativity will indeed make individuals rise—as individuals. But corporate animals have no individuality ("You can't afford to have friends on the way up."). The needs that such a man has can probably be partially filled by a reassessment of his values. The first step is voluntarily seeking help. But as with alcoholics, the first step—admitting the problem—is the hardest for such an individual to accept because in his sense of values it spells failure.

What is the cause or possible remedy? A sense of values consistent with individualism. Values are individual, not corporate. We have seen the result of corporate values. For example, one does not wait until after retirement to get a hobby, one develops an interest or passion during the prime of life and upon retirement becomes immersed in it.

The same with human values—it is a matter of human growth, tended during one's life, that allows one to develop a sense of human values and an individual identity—other than one of a metabolic or money-making machine. Why? Because the pursuit of material acquisition, which does give comfort, does not satisfy the spirit or soul. People with the success syndrome also have these needs. Because their spirit or soul lies fallow and undeveloped these people become bored with themselves. And they also successfully become agonizing bores to others. Being so utterly success oriented they must also be successfully boring.

What to do at this stage of life? Involve yourself in something other than yourself by developing an interest outside of yourself. Become aware. There are joys in areas other than competition. It is not easy for a person to begin doing new things at retirement. But it may well be worth the effort if your satisfactions in life, those which do not have a price tag on them, have worth. Who knows, these satisfactions may fill the vacuum of boredom with something other than alcohol. They may enable you to thrive on rarer air than you have been heretofore breathing. They may even remedy the situational impotence.

The moral of this chapter is—*Do* get to know your emotions. They are the keystone to your living and being. Get acquainted with them, closely, fearlessly. Being a friend to your emotions, rather than avoiding them as pests, will pay immense dividends to your physical, mental, and emotional well-being. It will avoid your entrapping yourself in situations such as those described in this chapter.

CHAPTER 15

The Unconscious and the Conscious

When we speak of the left-brain—right-brain dichotomy we are usually referring to its effect on our behavior. When we speak of the emotions, we are trying to probe the soil from which our behavior arises or the deep currents of feeling which lie under our conscious behavior. *This is the area of the unconscious.*

It is a land that has been much explored by psychologists, psychiatrists, sociologists, the religious fraternity, and especially the so-called mystics. However, while much explored, there has been comparatively little mined. And of that which has been mined, each school of thought has different interpretations. It is like an Indian bazaar. Each vendor has his little stand and hawks his psychological wares, each saying his way provides the key to inner knowledge. They cannot all be right. But we do not know which one is right. Each may be partially right. Or, all of them may be wrong.

But we have learned many things about the mind, though we may not know the mechanisms which produce them. We have learned that creativity is sparked or supported by hidden springs in the unconscious. (It was once called the subconscious—now known as the unconscious.) And we have learned that there is a stage of the unconscious that we call the preconscious. It is that area or time in which a sensation rises from the deeper domains of the unconscious toward the conscious—when we become aware of a thought, sensation, or finding.

All people are accustomed to dealing and doing things on the conscious level. Understandably, all scientific or technological, even artistic, work takes place when we are awake and concentrating on a task and accomplishing it. Even when we find our direction or experiment is wrong, we try to set it right in a fully conscious state. And in that state, too, we try to correct it or modify it so that it produces the result we hope or plan for.

But ideas, especially the creatives ones, arise on a level below the conscious. Unfortunately most people are not accustomed to, in fact often fear to, or perhaps do not even know how to let the mind wander in the unconscious. That is the landscape, if one can call it that, where our perceptions arise. It is there, where the outer limits of our perceptions wander.

Creativity has nothing to do with intelligence, which is a creature of the conscious, though the soil from which intelligence springs probably originates in the unconscious. Intelligence and creativity are different qualities. In the unconscious there are no boundaries, and one can soar in that area, not limited by the common sense of the mind or what the intellect calls rational. Instead, the unconscious deals with the *common sense of the soul* or spirit. This is the land of creativity where by some magic these impressions rise to a preconscious level and then find expression on the conscious level.

For example, the great German poet Friedrich Schiller (1759–1805) was told by another poet that the latter had dry periods in which he was not able to produce anything. Schiller, with uncanny prescience, told the inquiring poet that he was allowing his intellect to monitor or censor his imagination. The intellect is for the conscious product, it is the unconscious that develops the sensitized preconscious.

How acute are your perceptions? You can accentuate them by allowing them to roam, or acting on them to intensify creativity rather than to suppress it.

But many people have perceptual defenses. They do not dare to enter that land, which they can approach through daydreams or by allowing their minds to wander. Moreover, they have perceptual deafness. They don't hear that which they don't want to hear. For example, there was a novelist who had come to an impasse on the novel she was writing. She did not know how she could have one character bridge a given situation—make the transition leading into the next event. Many of the devices she had tried did not seem credible, most of them seemed contrived, probably because they were. How would this character get a specific idea, she mused? Once she figured it out, it would be clear sailing for the author.

Her editor advised her to use an occult device. That turned off the author. Then she was advised to have that specific idea come to the character in a dream. That, too, was rejected. The author was accustomed to dealing only in hard "realities" and felt uncomfortable with anything other than conscious machinations. Finally she was advised to have the character daydream and have the idea come to him as if he were in a reverie.

At first the author accepted the suggestion, since she had no other idea. But she quickly dropped it, giving as her reason that daydreams smack of the supernatural. Apparently "daydream" was a dirty word to her. She never was able to accept the idea that the wellspring of creativity lies in the unconscious. She did finally hit upon another device. Someone at a bar would give her character the idea on which he would act. For the character to accept the idea from "someone at a bar" on something that had to do with a personal and deeply felt conviction is perhaps the least credible solution. But the author was comfortable with it, as she did not have to deal with anything below the conscious.

Often ideas are taken in by the unconscious, buried there, forgotten but waiting to be summoned. They are transformed into another shape and are unknowingly used by the conscious mind, oblivious of their origin. The creative mind has an unerring sense of location of material, transforming it into something different, and exhuming it in another form.

For example, Freud believed he invented his method of free association in order to be able to elicit unconscious conflicts in his patients so that the patients would be able to verbalize them and bring them into the open. But Freud actually did not discover or invent the idea out of thin air. This method of writing down any thoughts or ideas about anything was originally proposed by the German author Ludwig Börne (1786–1837) to encourage fluency and fluidity in writers. Both Freud and Börne—although their objectives and uses were different—had very similar methods.

When this fact was brought to Freud's attention he had no recollection of having ever read Börne's book. But on searching he found that he had the book in his library— with marginal notes he'd made himself almost forty years before. The message was buried in his unconscious. It was transformed and exhumed in the form of free association practiced on the analyst's couch.

How do you enter the portals of the unconscious? It is the easiest and the hardest task. It is not a group endeavor. Group participation inhibits creative thinking. The portal to the unconscious is a door through which you enter alone. But it is not frightening. There is nothing to fear.

First, *trust your perceptions.* If you filter or censor your perceptions through your intellect you will strain out the spirit. Most likely you have splendid ideas buried in your unconscious—translate them into action by verbalizing them or writing them down, in short by doing something, acting. Above all, trust yourself. It does not matter that you may at first be wrong in your perceptions. What does matter is being comfortable with them, being comfortable with your perceptions. After you have allowed yourself to trust your perceptions, you will become comfortable with them, and you will find that they serve you well on the whole. Your judgment of people or ability to make decisions will improve and your creativity will develop and grow.

You may well be accustomed to linear thinking. Most people are until they become aware of the creative potential inherent in allowing the mind to soar. People unfortunately think in opposites: black vs. white; up vs. down; yes vs. no, does-she-or-doesn't-she. But comparatively few events are either/or propositions. They may be neither, they may be both. We discussed this in Part I.

CHAPTER 16

Meditation—Transcendental and Otherwise

Creativity is a potential with everyone. While this book is about creativity and not about meditation, psychological or parapsychological processes, some chapters are devoted to these techniques because they are related to creativity. The manner of their relation is this: Creativity springs from inner sources and resources. We should look into our inner resources and try to understand them.

We spoke of the emotions and the unconscious in the last three chapters. We discussed the noncreative and often up-tight posture of the quintessential businessman in the chapter before. At this point it would be sensible to consider how to reach the emotions—or the unconscious—or at least how to touch upon them.

There is no hard and fast rule, no rigid formula, which will give you the *Open Sesame* to these areas of the inner person. But there are a variety of approaches, some of which are feasible to practice without going off to a mountaintop to concentrate on your navel or sit and contemplate for the rest of your life.

One of the methods is meditation. But several questions suggest themselves. Meditate upon what? How long? How often? How do I know I am doing it right? Who can show me step by step how I can do it? And what can I expect from meditation? What will it do for me? What does it really have to do with creativity?

This chapter proposes to answer these questions about meditation. And more.

Meditation has been known for a long time, virtually

since man became somewhat more sophisticated than the savage. Virtually all religions include periods of meditation during which man contemplates his deities or God-like beings or even contemplates apparently inanimate subjects, as nature.

Meditation is an inner journey. It refreshes, it may inspire, it may produce revelations. It takes man out of the mundane and brings him into closer communion with the spiritual, the inner world of the soul. Meditation can help you to unwind and relax. Unfortunately, it can also bore the one who either fears to look into himself or has no inner resources from which to draw.

But above all: It has a potential for a great deal of good and it can do no harm. This is a rare situation, from the expectation that most good things can have side effects too. You know the common expectation—a medicine must taste bad before it can be good for you.

One type of meditation that has become extremely popular recently is one called *Transcendental Meditation,* usually referred to as TM. (Details are given further on in this chapter.) Another type of meditation is called the *Relaxation Response* (RR), which is virtually TM in a secular dress. TM does indeed have religious overtones to which some people object. Meditation is a secular form of Yoga, like contemplation broadly speaking, but with no ritual, no asceticism, no appeal to a higher being.

Which type of meditation is correct for you depends on your preference and emotional make-up. And depending on these, you will be able to make what will be the right choice for you.

But by all means, choose one—TM or RR. You will receive enduring and soaring benefits, not only in accentuating your creativity but also with respect to physical and emotional health. It is a substantially salubrious antidote to stress or distress, which is an unwanted part of the daily life.

About TM. I have taken the standard course of TM, given by SIMS (Students' International Meditation Society), which is under the aegis and the method of the Maharishi Mahesh Yogi. I entered the course like gangbusters to see what was wrong with it. I wanted to know if people were succumbing to a hoax. Was it another tulip craze of the Middle Ages, were people being taken in by another Mississippi Bubble? I came to scoff—and I stayed to pray, metaphorically speaking. I have fully described my experiences in a chapter. "TM Practice: A New Drug?" in a book edited by Martin Ebon and published by New American Library, *TM: How to Find Peace of Mind Through Meditation.*

And I am delighted to have taken the TM course. But later, I realized that one can teach the subject in less than an hour without the packaging and window dressing, which totals about eight hours. In fact, I have effectively taught others how to meditate in about half an hour.

TM effectively teaches meditation. It has a ritual that has a distinctly religious tone. The religion is Hinduism. The course is spread over four days of indoctrination, and finally an initiation into how to do it, at which time you repeat a word or phrase called a "mantra" silently to yourself as you meditate fifteen to twenty minutes at a time, twice a day. SIMS says that the mantra is specifically designed for you. I don't believe it. It is chosen from a specific list of words; many people have the same mantra.

Much of the original scientific investigation on the effects of TM was done by Dr. Herbert Benson, cardiologist, of Harvard Medical School, and Dr. Robert K. Wallace, psychologist. By a number of sophisticated methods they determined that TM has a distinct, wholesome physiological effect. Subsequently Dr. Benson, desiring to avoid the religious tone of TM yet to retain its beneficial effects, developed a virtually identical technique, which he called the *Relaxation Response,* and published a book under that name. (*See* reading list.)

My own belief is that there is no functional difference between TM or RR. Were I to know then what I know now, and were I to have had the RR available at the time I took the TM course. I would have chosen the RR and easily learned the technique from Benson's book. Nonetheless, I can readily concede that some people will have a preference for group instruction and the one-to-one encounter given by TM. It may give them more comfort to receive instruction by people trained by the Maharishi.

Now about RR: The RR method of meditation is done as follows:

1. Sit down in a comfortable position, preferably in a quiet place (though after having practiced RR you will be able to do it on the train, bus, or even sitting down in a corner—anywhere.) Relax. "Hang loose."

2. Close your eyes. Keep them closed, gently, don't force by squeezing your eyelids tightly. Do remember—this is for relaxation.

3. Relax. Mentally concentrate on relaxing your muscles. First begin at your feet, then go upward, a bit at a time—relaxing ankles, calves of your legs, knees, thighs, buttocks, your back and abdomen, chest and shoulders; do the same with your arms, wrists, fingers, and shoulders; next your neck, and finally your face. Relax. Savor the feeling of being relaxed. Your muscles will be now relaxed. Feel them un-tense. Loosen up, let your muscles go, release their tension. Relax. This whole process takes less than five minutes.

4. Then you breathe through your nose (your mouth will become dry if you breathe through it). Each time you breathe out you say to yourself, silently, the word "one"; *that is your mantra—"one."* Concentrate on hearing yourself say silently to yourself the mantra, "one" with each exhaled breath. Whenever a thought crosses your mind—and it will—drown it out with the mantra, "one." Think of your breathing, but above all, concentrate on your mantra. If your mantra escapes you—if you become conscious you haven't been saying "one" silently for a while, and another thought comes into your mind—don't worry. The mantra will come back. Just begin again saying it silently to yourself in rhythm with your exhaling. Above all, relax—don't try too hard. Easy does it best.

5. Keep this up for twenty minutes. To find out how long you have been at the meditation exercise, open your

eyes—gently—and look at the clock. *Do not* use the shock signal of an alarm clock. Soon you will discover that your body clocks itself. If you find you are only halfway through your twenty minutes, close your eyes and continue your meditation, repeating your mantra on each exhale.

6. At the end of your period of meditation sit quietly for a few minutes, then open your eyes slowly, and remain seated for a few more minutes. Do not get up suddenly— some people may possibly feel dizzy since meditation reduces blood pressure. Sudden moves, especially on arising, may possibly give you a slight but transient feeling of light-headedness due to lowered blood pressure.

It is recommended that meditation should not be done within two hours after eating. It may be well to follow that directive though none of the people with whom I discussed this point found it necessary to wait long after a meal.

Dr. Benson recommends the use of "one" as a mantra. In my own experience (and I have devised and used several other mantras) "one" is satisfactory provided that you pronounce it to rhyme with *bone*. Otherwise, one may think of the *numeral one* and may begin counting, two, three, four, etc., which could present a distraction. The objective of a mantra is to provide a sound that can be repeated, that has no meaning and therefore is not likely to set up a different trend of thought.

What does meditation do? What can it do for you?

Meditation, both TM and RR, produces a deep state of relaxation that is both mental and physical. It reduces metabolism—slows down the metabolic motor—hence creating a *hypo*metabolic state. And there is clear physiologic evidence that it does so.

For example, in an excited state a greater amount of oxygen is used by the body to supply the physiologic demands of the tissues. During meditation, and for a short time thereafter, less oxygen is used—the body needs less in this state. In fact, less oxygen is used during meditation than during sleep, indicative of a deeper sense of relaxation.

Commensurately, less carbon dioxide is exhaled during respiration. This is further indicative of the reduced metabolic rate; less oxygen is used hence less waste products are manufactured by the body—in this case carbon dioxide. These are clear indications of a slowdown of metabolism, or a reduced metabolic rate, a slowdown of the motor.

Blood pressure is reduced during meditation. This is broadly the opposite to a revved-up, or hyper, state. High blood pressure is hypertension. In fact, meditation is indeed used as an adjunct to the treatment of high blood pressure, which together with stomach ulcers, are the badges of the driving, overexcited state that frequently approaches the frenetic. Parallel with the reduction of blood pressure the heart rate is decreased, indicating a decreased work load on the heart.

There is another indication that meditation reduces tension—in this instance, anxiety. It is known that the level of lactic acid in the blood is increased by anxiety. Upon meditation there is a reduced level of lactic acid in the blood, a clear and objective measure of the reduction of anxiety. No wonder that meditation is conducive to relaxation.

The skin is the largest organ of man's body—and it is an organ, having its own characteristic metabolic functions. In fact, the skin aside from being a cover for the tissues is intimately involved in states of systematic disease. Many diseases, including hepatitis, some cancers, certain nervous disturbances, show signs on the skin. For that reason the skin has often been called the *mirror of disease*.

One of the ways in which internal reactions are reflected on the skin is by the electrical resistance it exhibits. Broadly speaking, an increased skin resistance is parallel with relaxation and a lowered one with tension. Concurrent with meditation, there is an increased electrical resistance of the skin, indicative of relaxation. That is an objective test, and objectivity is virtually venerated in our current philosophy.

One of the important tests related to relaxation, and indirectly to creativity, has to do with brain waves that are recorded by an electroencephalograph. Many investigations have found that one of the brain waves—the alpha brain wave—is increased with meditation. Some investigators report an increase of alpha waves gives evidence of deep relaxation and is also associated with creative endeavors. Relaxation associated with one of the stages of creativity is a positive note.

For those reasons, meditation is a tremendously helpful influence in the treatment or amelioration of disease conditions that are sparked by or associated with tension. It has been used in hypertension or high blood pressure, bronchial asthma, sleeplessness, low back pain, muscle spasm, "jitteriness," or any of the manifestations of nervous tension. Meditation has also curbed drug abuse and has been used successfully as an adjunct in the treatment of a number of other conditions. Emotionally tense people have muscle spasms, relaxation is a preeminent answer to those spasm.

In addition to the benefits you may receive if you are prone to these conditions, meditation will augment your calm and reduce your irritability—in other words, it may well make you easier to live with. Meditation should magnify your perception in that you will have taken one step on your inner journey. Perhaps for that reason it should magnify your learning ability. With increased perception you should be more observant or alert. And above all, meditation will expand your calm in the jungle-like atmosphere of modern living.

Predominantly TM and some other forms of relaxation as well are not the products of charlatans. The effects of meditation have been studied in respectable institutions such as university laboratories, at Stanford Research Institute, and other research installations.

Is TM or RR used by people other than the counterculture? The relaxation methods are used now in a broad spectrum of the population, including executives of Arthur D. Little, Inc., a highly respected creative research organization.

One hot-shot businessman, the president of an important company who had planned to learn and practice relaxation, hesitated. He asked, "If I practice relaxation, will this reduce my tremendous drive?"

What this man needed was to take a deep look into his own values not a method of relaxation. He needed to learn how to be comfortable with being more efficient with less anxiety, for such super drives create anxiety and the problems associated with it. He didn't know that often when you relax and let go, you gain more.

Perhaps this man's limited values can be best epitomized by the story pertaining to a conversation between an immensely greedy businessman and his partner, a man who had focus and a sense of values beyond that of a money-making machine.

The partner with some sense of values asked: "We have 58 per cent of the market on our product. Why are you moving heaven and earth to get more?"

The greedy partner replied: "Because we don't have 98 per cent of the market."

That is what William James, great American psychologist, must have meant when he said, "Success is the bitch goddess," demanding eternal enslavement.

Stop a moment—pick spiritual daisies.

(*See* Chapter 18, "Stress and the Mode of Living," and Chapter 12, "Business and Loyalty.")

CHAPTER 17

The Sixth, Seventh Senses

If the topics of the previous two chapters on the unconscious and meditation appear to you to be witch medicine, relax. Witch medicine often works when other measures fail. It's all in the mind, you say? Of course. So are memory, thinking, planning, and other mentally or emotionally triggered tasks.

In fact, so is creativity. The whole purpose of this chapter is to explain how valuable having an open mind *can be*—for you and your creativity. The objective is to get into the mind, whether you want to explore what makes you or someone else creative, or how you can accentuate creativity in order to raise your own or someone else's self-esteem and values and convert boredom into contented productivity.

That is the reason we should consider briefly what is on the other side of the veil in the never-never magic land of faith healing, metapsychiatry, ESP (extra-sensory perception), psychic phenomena, cosmic influences. All these are in the mind, beyond the mind, and in the external world that plays the chords of your internal worlds. *Much can be mined if the mind is open*. This pun is intended—to act as a mnemonic to help you remember this concept, expecially if you have been devoted to the stuff called "facts." *Veneration of facts is gross idolatry*.

And I am not at all suggesting that you become a zealot in this area. Dogma or zealotry at any end of the spectrum is deplorable. It clouds your vision for the whole picture. The point is to keep the heart and mind open, we may learn something in the process. We can also position ourselves to absorb the auras of creativity. We shall be going over this tremendous subject only lightly, to show you that the world you know not only exists but is also worthy of respectful attention and supplemental reading. Don't let your preconceptions, your foregone conclusions on these "mystical things" close your mind and heart. *Your creativity may be at stake.*

You may have been accustomed to command your senses. Shift over into the right hemisphere of your brain. Make your senses talk to you. What you are trying to do in enlarging your creative potential is to reach the deeper strata within you. You are trying to turn over the topsoil and reach the deeper soil underneath. This is just contrary to the often accustomed way of covering up, metaphorically speaking—sweeping problems under the rug. Then we tend to put concrete on the top. In doing so we seal off the streams of creativity.

Each of the topics briefly to be touched upon here affects creativity. Your whole objective is to relax enough so that when streams of creativity begin to trickle through or come up like a springs, you will recognize them, nurture them rather than push them away. And you will begin to welcome them and be comfortable with them.

Perhaps an illustration will explain this point graphically: everyone knows that a large part of Manhattan Island is made up of swamps with rivers, springs, and wells underneath. The skyscrapers have been built only in places where there is solid bedrock. What we have done in building New York City is to encase it in a concrete shell, even some front and back yards have been cemented over. Thus New York is all head and no body, and any rumble from the body underneath cannot come through the concrete shell. By analogy, unless we dig deeper in ourselves, our psyches, no creative rumble will come through. We have to break the concrete shell to let matters of the spirit emerge. With Hamlet, we can paraphrase, *There are more things in this world, Horatio, than are apparent to our five senses.* And these clearly influence our five senses.

Our typical Western approach is to investigate phenomena "scientifically" always with a "rational" approach. But while we are only investigating phenomena, the Russians are applying them and using them for practical purposes.

For example, take Kirlian photography. Originally observed and developed by a Russian couple, Semyon and Valentina Kirlian, we have known about this technique for some time but considered it just a rather interesting phenomenon and put it on the back burner. In the meantime the Russians have been successfully using it to diagnose diseases, states of well-being of human organisms, and following progress in treatment.

Kirlian photography is unlike standard photographic methods. Using no camera lenses, a part of a body, such as a finger, is placed close to unexposed film in the dark and the whole put between two metal plates. A light electrical charge is turned on. The result is a photograph that shows an aura, a halo, or a corona around the part of the body thus photographed. The aura is in brilliant colors reflecting the state of mental, emotional, or physical conditions in the subject photographed. Think of flares in the sun, an aurora borealis translated onto a much smaller scale—these are like the auras around people. The image shown in Kirlian photography probably reflects the human unseen energy field around man.

The outstanding exponent and investigator of Kirlian photography in the U.S. is Dr. Thelma Moss, psychologist, of the University of California of Los Angeles. She reports that Kirlian photographs strikingly reflect conditions of relaxation as induced by meditation, hypnosis, and even drugs, as well as tension and excitement—all of which are emotional states. Dr. Moss states that "vibes" between people may be real, as subjects photographed react differently to different photographers taking Kirlian photographs.

As recently as ten years ago cosmic influences, magnetic forces, and astrology were cited as preeminent examples of superstitition. Fortunately, the minds of the Establishment and of science are being opened a chink.

For example, nose and throat surgeons in Tallahassee, Florida, reported that hemorrhages from nose and throat operations are 82 per cent higher in the moon's second quarter than at any other time. Magic? Superstition? Apparently not. We are merely opening our minds a bit to something we can not yet explain.

Despite the calumny heaped upon it, the American Medical Association has been a considerable force for good. Yet, toward unorthodox methods and beliefs pertaining to health and medicine, it has been an unremitting foe, in that way discouraging any ventures that do not support the status quo of medicine.

It is therefore surprising and gratifying that the august AMA has opened the pages of one of its publications to what has been considered witch medicine. Its publication, *Today's Health,* carried an article, "Cosmic Influences May Determine Career Choices," of which the following is an abstract.

If Mars was at its zenith when your baby was born does that mean he might become a great doctor?

Of course not.

But then on the other hand . . .

An article in the October [1971] *Today's Health,* the general circulation magazine of the American Medical Association, discusses some recent findings that may support this dream.

Michel Gauquelin, an investigator in the field of biomagnetics, which evaluates the effect of the earth's magnetic field on animal life, discovered a surprising correlation between the position of the planets when great men were born and their occupations.

Eminent doctors whom he studied showed an unaccountable statistical preference for being born during the day when either Mars or Saturn had just risen or was at its zenith.

Interestingly, the discovery was made during the course of an investigation into astrology, which proved conclusively that astrology could not predict the future. In the course of investigating the lives of 25,000 men from all over Europe, the scientist found that certain occupations were clustered around specific planets:

Mars and Saturn for doctors, Jupiter for actors, and the moon for writers.

The researcher suggests that the magnetic forces of a heavenly body may act on a particular genetic code— the magnetic ray acting as a "releaser" at birth.

Still other researchers have noticed other effects of biomagnetics:

The composition of human blood can be altered by sunspots.

Psychiatric admissions increase during magnetic storms.

One of the pioneers in this controversial branch of biology, Giorgi Piccardi, discovered that many different chemical reactions vary according to the magnetic influences of the 11-year sunspot cycle. He also learned that March and September will affect these reactions as well.

Within the last five years a number of investigators have shown that a wide variety of organisms, ranging from birds to insects, respond sensitively to the earth's very weak magnetic field.

Serious investigators in the field are impatient with what they call the "mystics" of the field of biomagnetics. Scientists feel these people are too eager to assign a wide range of diseases, including mental illness, to sunspots and other disturbances of the magnetic field of the earth. But as the effects of biomagnetics are charted, it becomes more apparent that the field shows a great potential for having profound effects on politics, history, sociology and medicine.

The importance of magnetic influences on human life has long been known. How? We are not sure, but fossil records tell the highlights of the story that life has been at least disrupted and almost destroyed on this planet over and over many times in the past. Some animal species have become extinct during upheavals that have taken place about six times—500, 425, 345, 250, 180 and 65 *million years ago*. (Note: the extraordinary disclosures of Immanuel Velikovsky, who has been cruelly attacked by scientists, are now being shown to be right in an increasing number of instances—following the extraorbital launchings of spacecraft.)

The probable reason for these near extinctions of life on earth correlates well with a reduction to zero of the magnetic field. (The magnetic field is reduced to zero before it builds up again.) When it is low, and especially at zero, there is no protection against cosmic radiation.

The artillery of the scientific establishment has always been brought out against diagnosis and healing by other than orthodox means. Sometimes it appears as if the principal objective of the medical establishment has been to maintain the status quo of medicine and the unquestioned majesty of the physician rather than the care of the sick. That this suppresses creativity in medicine is clear. In the unrelenting and incessant attack against most fully new ideas, medicine has forgotten that even if a new discovery turns out to be wrong it is a gain because the succeeding approach developed from the "wrong idea" may lead one into regions that are extraordinary advances. The scientific establishment welcomes building upon established ideas or innovations, but it is unremitting in its hostility to new, creative ideas. It attacks under the banner of scientific basis and at times makes itself the laughing stock a generation later.

A fine example of hostility to something new took place in 1842. In an operating theater before the Baltimore Medico-Chirurgical Society there was a planned demonstration of a leg being amputated. *The only anesthetic used was hypnosis.* The patient reported that he was comfortable during the operation and said that he had felt no pain during the amputation.

The elite—the notable establishment surgeons—were present at the operation. It was indeed something new. Painless amputation of a leg? Impossible. *Click-shut* went their minds. But how did they explain the phenomenon to themselves and to each other? All were eyewitnesses. It was decided that the patient had had excruciating pain, which was expected, but that he had kept silent *because he wanted to please his surgeon!*

The surgeons present would never accept the idea that the mind can change reality, even when they were witnesses to a perfect example—their own behavior. The reality of the patient's own statement could not be accepted, so their minds made their own absurd reality.

Today, hypnosis is accepted as a reality that works in many areas—for relaxation, to alleviate anxiety and apprehension, to treat habits such as smoking and overeating, which a person desires to overcome. It is also used to improve dysfunctions associated with sexual disorders, and to treat conditions that are believed to arise from the psyche or emotions, such as certain skin conditions, even to get rid of warts.

But our interest in creativity makes us want to look into another area with respect to hypnosis. Some people intensely fear it. Why? The reason gives us some insights as to why people suppress creativity and virtually fear it.

Fear is one of the reasons people refuse to use hypnosis toward the solution of a problem that they want to ameliorate. Hypnosis is a method of eliciting or evoking mental content. Do they fear being found empty? They say they fear that they will "lose control" of themselves, though they are never clear what they mean by that phrase. Another fear people have is *a fear of surrender*. But people don't think this through: The very act of going to a singles bar is a form of surrender that has clear dangers (à la Judith Rossner's novel *Looking For Mr. Goodbar*). Yet the same women who go to those places because they are lonely would not think of *surrender* in the form of hypnosis. Their fear of surrender covers any condition and all circumstances in any event. (The fact that they may have surrendered to a noxious habit such as overeating does not occur to them.)

Another point of which people are often oblivious is that *love is mutual surrender*.

Here is an apparent correlation: it has been observed that those who cannot receive love also cannot give love. They can accept love passively, even graciously, but they cannot give love, either of their own volition or return love. Similarly, creativity demands surrender of heretofore accepted or practiced doings and events if they are not consistent with the surges of creativity. *Surrender does not necessarily mean loss.*

Another example that has called down upon it the wrath of the establishment is psychic healing. There have been in the past—and also at present—glaring examples of fraud in this area. Fakery begins with the gypsy who switches a handkerchief in which a gullible woman has tied all her money for purposes of having it "blessed" and gives her a look-alike one—not to be opened for some weeks—containing cut-up newspaper. It extends to charlatans who draw thousands with promises to heal. Between these extremes there are dozens of operators who prey on people. And yet, there are genuine healers.

But how can you tell the mountebank from the psychic healer? It is difficult. Since some scientists, as Dr. Bernard Grad of McGill University, and Dr. C. Norman Shealey of the University of Wisconsin, have come into the medical press, it is becoming easier to do it. And an increasing number of reputable scientists and physicians are publishing reports on psychic healing.

Psychic healing is an overall term to designate the curing of a person by a healer who claims some form of psychic power or energy inherent in him that enables him to diagnose a problem, or through which he heals the sick person by transferring his psychic energy. Psychic healing does not necessarily claim to come from supernatural powers.

Item: Dr. Grad had intentionally induced burns on the skin of a number of rats. One group of rats were left as a control group. Another group of rats in a cage were held in the hands of a healer for a short period each time. It became clear to observers that the wounds of the rats held by the psychic healer healed considerably quicker than those who were not held but kept as controls. Grad also demonstrated a more rapid sprouting of barley seeds held by the healer than those not held.

Item: Dr. C. Norman Shealey states that psychics can diagnose some illnesses from complaints given to them as accurately as physicians without risk entailed in X rays or other sophisticated modern methods. He studied two hundred patients for eighteen months who had been correctly diagnosed by psychics—three out of four times. This is about the same degree of accuracy as those of physicians.

There were a number of various psychics who were utilized in the study. They included astrologers, palmists, numerologists, clairvoyants. Most of them did not see the patient, nor did most of them receive medical information. The clairvoyants used photographs of the patients, astrologers and numerologists used birthdates, the palmists used palm prints. Dr. Shealey further says that when three psychics agree, "you can get an accuracy of 98 percent, and that's much better than we doctors can do."

Item: Arigo, a Brazilian peasant who had never studied medicine or even gone beyond the third grade, treated up to three hundred patients daily. He successfully performed surgery in a matter of minutes, with knives, scissors, and with his hands, without antiseptics or anesthetics. Patients from all over the world came to him—some with fatal diseases. He operated as if in a trance, and he claimed to be guided by the spirit of a German physician, long dead, whom Arigo had never known. His work has been observed and filmed by American and other physicians. Did the claimed cures take places? There is documentary evidence to that effect. What is the explanation for these extraordinary events? Unknown.

Mind Over Cancer?

Cancer is a disease dreaded by everyone. There is a considerable amount of evidence that the mind can make one cancer prone, and other evidence of the disappearance of a tumor by mental ministration. (Cancers have also been known to regress spontaneously—without any apparent help—but rarely. Apparently, the mind can change reality, but what reality are we talking about?)

Is cancer a reality?

Can a *stiff upper lip* give you cancer?

Can the mind make you cancer prone?

Human cancer may be the result of a last-ditch creative act, performed by the body in response to a frustrated emotional need for self-esteem.

Is cancer psychosomatic? Extraordinary? Note this: Emotional stress and mental illness may be immunological disturbances and there is evidence that resistance to cancer may be immunologic.

Contradictory? Not at all, because the emotional status affects the immunological or resistance-producing nature of the body, as will be detailed further on. This is not much different from the psychosomatic aspects of other diseases; ulcerative colitis, stomach ulcers, high blood pressure, asthma, and even rheumatoid arthritis have long carried large or small labels that read: *psychosomatic*.

The above are reports of studies on the psychologic aspects of cancer in which three hundred investigators collaborated at the Second Conference on the Psychophysiological Aspects of Cancer, in May 1968 sponsored by the New York Academy of Sciences.

Are we discussing a new treatment of cancer? Not at all—emotional aspects are not direct but contributing causes. The reason this topic will be detailed is to sharpen the concept that the mind has a role in the function of what were previously considered extraordinary happenings.

That the mind has a key role in creativity is not doubted. This chapter has two purposes: (1) to show the extent of the influence of and on the mind, and (2) to prepare the reader for the next chapter, on stress. Stress indeed has a key role in creativity. According to some, stress itself may trigger the mind to break out in a creative endeavors, thereby ameliorating stress. Others believe, and they are in the majority, that stress suppresses the creative effort. In fact, both may be right—at different times.

Why do some people develop cancer and others exposed to the same influences—smoking, pollution, family history of cancer, etc.—do not? The asnwer is not easy or apparent. But that it has to do with the *resistance* of the organism is not disputed. And resistance can be variously defined or interpreted. Resistance can apply to susceptibility to many disease conditions or disturbances. However, currently, resistance is defined on an immunologic basis.

Immunology deals with susceptibility to or security against a disease-producing agent, a disease, or poison to the system. In short, it has to do with resistance to or protection against disease. Resistance deals with the ability of the body to ward off (resist) disease-producing effects of bacteria, viruses, or other agents, including toxins that produce a disease condition.

We are familiar with germs and other microorganisms causing disease. But we do not as readily accept the concept that mental or emotional states can produce disease. This idea becomes more familiar when we recollect that excitement and sustained pressure on the person are one of the causes of hypertension or high blood pressure.

Similarly, mental and emotional distresses upset the hormonal balance in the body and thus lessen resistance. Dr. Claus B. Bahnson, professor of psychiatry at the Medical School of Jefferson University in Philadelphia, has been in the vanguard in the study of psychopathology of cancer. According to his findings, an upset of the balance of hormones in the body may affect the immunologic process and may produce susceptibility to cancer. He states that denial and repression of emotion since childhood, and especially after personal loss and tragedy with a failure to express grief, causes internalization rather than expression of emotions and that such repressions may produce susceptibility to cancer.

And he is not alone in this position. Dr. Lawrence L. Leshan of the Institute of Applied Biology in New York City in his study of seven hundred patients with cancer states that, "Bleak hopelessness about ever attaining any meaning, zest, or validity in life . . ." is much more common in cancer than in noncancer patients. Lost relationships, which meant much to the individual, are also significant.

Many questions suggest themselves. Does giving up precede onset of cancer? Cancer is said to be rare in schizophrenics; is it because they have escaped the stresses of life by escaping into insanity?

Stressful emotions lead to various diseases, the stomach ulcer in the high-powered executive is well known. But the largest problem is that stress leads to chronic diseases if one lives with the damaging emotions for a long time. The reason is that stress lowers resistance by continuous contact. While unpleasant emotions are generally unhealthy, two of them—anger and fear—are the most damaging. They release a potent hormone, adrenaline. A continous exposure to adrenaline is most damaging. Anger and fear, in effect, create psychological wounds. Other substances are also mobilized or released by emotional upset. Dr. P. V. Cardon of the National Institutes of Health found that fat may be mobilized psychogenically. He reports that, "Psychic [psychological] phenomena can lead to large and rapid mobilization of free fatty acids . . . which is often abnormally elevated in patients with active cancer. Elevation of free fatty acids may pressage tumor activity."

Dr. George F. Solomon of Stanford University also found a likely relationship, and he cautiously reports: "Stress, emotional distress, may influence the function of the immunological system and environmental and psychological factors may in some instances be implicated as pathogens of cancer."

At the University of London, Medical Faculty, Dr. Graham Bennette states somewhat more baldly, "Invasive cancer is seen as a pathological condition allowed to proceed through failure of psychobiological control." It is no wonder that he concludes, "[a] cancer patient is typically emotionally isolated." And also: "The guilt of alienation is the failure of love."

Elsewhere doctors Marjorie B. and Claus Bahnson recount that according to a test they developed (Bahnson Rhythmical Apperception Test) they "predict that cancer patients make use of repression and denial of ego defenses in order to cope with psychological conflicts related to loss, hostility, and *creativity*." (Emphasis supplied.)

The clearest statement was made, paradoxically enough, by Sigmund Freud: *"We must love in order not to fall ill, and must fall ill, when, in consequence of neurosis, we cannot love."*

It is not new that psychic factors can change biochemical states and produce physiological states (blushing, blanching, etc.). When continued and noxious, they can affect the body's control mechanisms and lead to chronic disease. Thus, emotions play a role in susceptibility to disease, including infectious diseases, when immunological mechanisms lower resistance.

One of the most destructive emotions is depression. Boredom, previously mentioned in several different contexts, often and quite commonly leads to depression. The boredom and depression of retirement are quite common. What is not as often considered is that still fully active people may find themselves bored after work; work itself or alone does not fully fulfill. What do you do after work?

The problem is compounded with the push to greater leisure by unions and do-good organizations. Many people do not know what to do with the leisure they now have after work or on weekends, and they slowly die of boredom. How will they fill the extra leisure, which may become a reality if the three-day work week should become an unfortunate reality?

If you find lacks in your life you may find that some form of creativity will open new vistas to you. You must be aware of the *whole picture* otherwise the form of creativity you may choose may become occupational therapy without joy or fulfillment.

The whole picture includes reassessment of your personal interrelationships. The overachiever is often a pathetic underachiever in interpersonal or intrafamilial relationships.

In that reassessment, communication is an indispenable component. *The opposite of communication is not silence but alienation.* The pathology of alienation dams up emotional discharges. In this chapter a grave possibility—cancer—was related to alienation. True, not everyone gets cancer. But most people get a *horror vacuui*—fear of boredom—unless they are creatively engaged, a royal remedy for boredom and dissatisfactions with the world.

PSI PHENOMENA

These so called extranormal conditions or phenomena—as parapsychology, ESP, precognition, clairvoyance, psychokinesis, etc.—are known under the umbrella term of *psi phenomena*.

Psi has to do with communication. But what sort of communication? It is communication by thought, not by the normal five senses of seeing, hearing, tasting, touching, smelling.

Since this book is about creativity, why take up psi phenomena? Because *creativity lies beyond the five senses, though it may be triggered by one of them,* as sight or smell for example. Psi is thus related to creativity. For example, foreseeing something before it happens is another expression of our preconscious, where many creative ideas arise.

Here is a brief glossary of psi terms, which will give you a glimpse of creativity beyond the five senses:

Clairvoyance   —Knowing about an event that is occurring at a distance without seeing it, such as calling out a symbol on a playing card that someone else has chosen.

ESP   —Extra-sensory perception. Reading someone's mind, especially at a distance, the so-called sixth sense; presumably an energy exchange between the minds of two people.

Metapsychiatry   —The interface or meeting place between psychiatry and mysticism.

Precognition   —Foretelling, or prophecy; recognizing an event that will occur before it happens.

Psychokinesis   —Influencing a physical event to occur, as say, having dice come up in a combination one strongly wills to happen, or moving a physical object by thought without physical help.

Telesomatic   —Perception at a distance of an illness that occurs in another, usually a close person.

If you are unfamiliar with this area I suggest that you become acquainted with it, it may help you extend your mind or your spirit. In the reading list at the end of the book there are a number of books dealing with the paranormal. If a given book is published in paperback I have listed the paperback edition in preference to the more expensive hardcover edition.

In the appendix you will also find the names and addresses of foundations or institutions dealing with subjects beyond the five senses. I have selected those which I know or which are known to be reputable.

To paraphrase again, in summary: "There are more things in this world Horatio, *than are apparent to your meager senses.*" (See chapter 13 *Right Brain-Left Brain;* Chapter 25 *Science and Insight;* See Appendix "What Does One Do For Fun?)

CHAPTER 18

Stress and the Mode of Living

This book is about creativity. We have discussed other conditions, states, topics, or events because each of them is obviously and clearly related to creativity. Either evoking it or suppressing it. For that reason, too, the manner of healing or dealing with a noxious influence, such as stress, properly should be considered. Creativity implies *a letting go*. It includes letting one's mind wander—and hopefully to soar. To help you or condition you *to be able* to let go, there are chapters in this book on how-to-do-it. One of them, among others, is on meditation. There are other and more complex ways of letting go, as hypnosis, autogenic training, biofeedback.

This chapter is devoted to the other side of the coin, namely holding back, *not letting go* i.e. stress. Stress is any situation—physical, mental, or particularly emotional—that is threatening to us. It may be threatening physically, or it may threaten our familial or environmental security, or our mental or emotional tranquility.

Don't repeat the tired cliché, "A little stress is good for me." How much is a little, and when? While one cannot escape some stress when living—even in crossing the street—we cope with it, usually adequately. Even anticipating a letter for which you may have been waiting a week or more that does not come is mildly stressful. But that is the kind of stress you don't take steps to avoid. The point is this: The stresses in life, minor and major, have to be handled, and coping mechanisms have to be used. As to major stresses, the ideal remedy is prevention. *But before one can prevent anything one must recognize what one wants to prevent.* And only you can determine what is stress and what is distress for you.

Agents that produce stress vary with people. To some, the anticipation of sexual relations can be stressful, leading to impotence and other symptoms in men and equally undesirable effects in women, such as revulsion toward contact with a given man, developing into antipathy toward men especially in the sexual context.

Stress produces disease—physical and emotional. Emotional tensions—anxiety, fear, particularly anger—are the most powerful stress agents, and they can lead to diseases of the heart, digestive, and other vital organs. As Dr. Bruce Ogilvie, psychiatrist at San Jose (California) University puts it, "We are losing some of the nation's best businessmen, scientists, and scholars to stress. Hard work, utter dedication, self-sacrifice may not result in happiness and joy, but it is most efficient in producing stress."

Does that mean stop being thoroughly involved in work? Not at all. But it does mean a broadening of interests and dedication. The aim is *coping* with stress.

Stresses will manifest themselves as disease unless an adequate coping mechanism has been developed. And disease often is heralded by stress, which precedes disease by one or two years. *In that fashion stress is a predisease state.*

Profound stresses are disorganizing. Different people may consider different events more or less stressful, but certain events such as old age or grief are commonly stressful to everyone. Loss produces separation anxiety or grief, both pronouncedly stressful; unemployment is quite stressful because here there is a feeling of loss of control, and work is looked upon as a symbol of masculine identity.

Even mice show social stress by developing hypertension, as reported by Dr. James P. Henry. It is induced by overcrowding, territorial conflicts, isolation early in life, even such events as a cat in the room, though safely in different cages.

According to doctors Meyer Friedman and Ray H. Rosenman, authors of *Type A Behavior and Your Heart,* our behavior patterns are killing us. The road to well-being, according to them, is not greased with "a little margarine" instead of butter, but the road to heart attack is greased by stress. Type A behavior: This is the pattern of the hard-driving overachiever, like the successful and dynamic businessman, who works hard and plays hard.

Similarly, Dr. Samuel Silverman, professor of psychiatry at Harvard University School of Medicine, ascribes to stress most physical and other illnesses. He states that, "Stress always precedes the onset of physical symptoms, though stress does not inevitably lead it." Silverman has gained a national reputation in his accurate prediction of the pardoned Richard Nixon's phlebitis and subsequent embolism. The illness would be physical, said Silverman, because Nixon keeps tightly reined within himself any emotional expression. The legs, reasoned Silverman, would be the target organs because of Nixon's previous phlebitis, and also the lung due to previous pneumonia. Nixon had a lung embolism less than a week after the onset of phlebitis.

Stress is often a constant companion in business organizations. It reduces employee health and surely efficiency. If employers were to use a broader outlook rather than tunnel vision it would be clear to them, in the interest of intelligent selfishness, that stress is the worst enemy of business because it bores from within an organization. And often it is fully avoidable. At times an employee has to be fired. While it creates stress with other employees, it may well be a necessary part of the conduct of a firm. But communication and explanations to the other employees reduce their stress. There is no fear like the unknown.

For example, rumors were floating in the air of a large business organization that a wide-reaching change in administration was imminent. The manager of one important department advised some of the top executives on a Friday what the changes would be, and at the same time announced to the rest of the staff that he would not inform them until Monday morning what the large-scale changes were to be. His act as a manager was probably not sadistic but utter thoughtlessness or stupidity, in forcing his large staff to freeze and fry for the weekend, creating a tremendous stress until Monday. That Monday, and for the next two days, there was little work done despite the fact that the change affected only two people, and at that mildly.

Many of the stresses in business that usually can be avoided are produced by thoughtlessness on the part of managers, by depersonalization at a job, and by a lack of understanding on the part of management. For example, management often feels that if employees fail to show emotion they are secure and all is well. But management is unaware that in our society a show of emotion, except for anger, is equated with weakness. To gain the impression of being "strong," people take on the posture of the *strong and silent* type. Little do they realize that management nearsightedly prefers the strong and silent posture believing that such people can be handled or manipulated more easily without disruption. It is the old manipulation behind the concept of free will, which engenders guilt.

Among physically induced stressor agents are extreme cold or heat, pain, injuries such as burns, surgery, infections, disturbances of the biological rhythm engendered by rapid transportation, especially supersonic flight between different time zones producing jet lag.

All change is stressful. And change is an immutable event in life. Living carries its normal stresses—a sure sign that you are alive. Even pleasant changes, such as marriage, buying a home, etc., can be productive of stress.

Dr. Thomas H. Holmes prepared a Social Readjustment Rating Scale, a table of various activities giving a relative value of stresses produced by various changes. There were some startling results. For example, the death of a spouse is on top of the column for stress production with an arbitrary value of 100. While children leaving home rates 29 on the scale, marriage rates as considerably more stressful with an assigned value of 47. Even marital reconciliation is about equally stressful with a value of 45. Divorce is naturally more stressful with a value of 73. Unusual personal achievement might be assumed to be all fun and no stress. Not so. Success carries a stress rating of 28.

More prononuncedly stress-producing is a feeling of despair and loss of hope that expresses itself in helplessness.

For example, if an individual is placed in a nursing home without options at choosing whether to stay in his home or go to an old age residence, a feeling of helplessness is engendered. We all want to be captains of our own ships and *loss of choice kills all semblance of control.* This leads to the greatest of all stresses, namely, *giving up.*

The state of giving up is the forerunner of death. It has been observed, among others symptoms, to precede death in cancer and other patients. Symbols also can produce stress and death. For example, put a cat near a mouse, and stress is produced in the mouse—manifested by hypertension—*although both are safely in separate cages.* Symbols can be as powerful as tangible dangers.

One type of death from a symbol is well known—death by voodoo incantation, provided the victim *knows* he is being prayed to death. Another type of death, where a snake is the symbol, has been described (GP Edit. 19; 79; March 1959) wherein an individual died of fright from snakebite, though he was bitten by a nonpoisonous snake. Death occurred because it was expected, and the victim gave up.

The mechanism by which these deaths occurred is the psychological shock that produced a metabolic change in the body incompatible with life. In those instances there was a massive discharge of hormones from the autonomic system, probably adrenaline.

The whole concept of psychosomatic medicine is based on the knowledge that psychic or emotional conditions produce clear body or somatic responses. For example, Dr. Milton S. Grossman of the National Pituitary Agency of the University of Maryland School of Medicine reported that emotional deprivation strikingly interfered with the function of the pituitary, the master gland, by producing pituitary insufficiency. Hence children may turn out to be badly undersized due to reduced amounts of growth hormone produced by the pituitary as a result of emotional deprivation.

Dr. Hans Selye, world authority on stress, who evolved the General Adaptation Syndrome, has devoted his whole life to investigating the biochemical aspects of stress. He has done a tremendous amount of work on the biochemical explanation of psychically or emotionally triggered stress.

Dr. Selye also demonstrated another aspect—how certain chemicals are stressor agents. For example, blood sugar rises with stress as stress stimulates the release of adrenaline in the body, which in turn stimulates the secretion of glucose (sugar) by the liver thus raising blood sugar. Anxiety, a stressful condition, and more especially anger or depression increase the level of free fatty acids (FFA), mobilizing them from fat deposits into the bloodstream, as reported by Dr. Peter Mueller of the National Institutes of Health.

Dr. Robert J. Haggerty, professor of public health at the Harvard School of Public Health well summarized the relation of stress to human disease. "Experienced clinicians know that some families have more than their share of illness and frequently these seem to be the same families who experience a great deal of stressful events. . . . Recently a good deal of information has been accumulated showing that acute and chronic stress in families is associated with greater frequency of a wide variety of illnesses. There is also evidence that visits to medical care providers are increased after family stress, independent of the amount of illness. The nature of the stressing event varies, but most commonly includes death of near relatives, job loss or change, moves, trouble in school, work, marriage, or difficulties with the law."

Reviewing research findings on the mechanisms by which stress works to increase susceptibility to disease, Dr. Haggerty cited observations that "there is a widespread biologic phenomenon of increased susceptibility to disease when people do not get feedback that their reactions are leading to desirable or anticipated consequences. A lack of supportive environment at times of stressful events as well as previous life experiences in receiving realistic feedback seem to be major variables in why some respond to stress by increased risk of illness or inappropriate use of health services and others do not. Animal research has also shown a variety of physiologic changes when stress is not mitigated by a supportive environment."

Other examples: Stressful emotions cause an aggregation of blood platelets, this can lead to clotting and heart attack. The body loses a great deal of vitamin C during stress; for this reason vitamin C is called the stress vitamin. Stress enlarges the adrenal glands, which lose vitamin C during stress as amply demonstrated by Dr. Selye.

It is folk knowledge that whenever we are badly frightened—a powerful stress-producing emotion—diarrhea occurs. Mice have been repeatedly shown to defecate, demonstrated with other animals too, by being suddenly brought into a new environment. Change is stressful in various frameworks.

"Unhappiness causes lowered resistance," says authority on tuberculosis, Dr. G. Day. This is not extraordinary, as stress partially immobilizes the immunologic system.

But how can stress be handled? What can you do to lessen its effects? Any organism, human or otherwise, meeting a noxious or stressful situation must cope or succumb. It copes by adapting to the stress, or it dies. Easily said, but how to do it?

Coping mechanisms or adaptive behavior to psychological stress take various forms. It must be reasonably satisfying to the individual for otherwise it is not an adequate coping mechanism. For example, when we are living in a considerably stressful situation it is easy to say, "Don't worry about it." But this advice is worse than useless because it is also irritating to the individual under stress. It is marvelous to have a change of attitude, and to ignore stress, but it is not often realistic.

Naturally, the type of stress must be first considered, it may need medical or psychiatric intervention. For example, an individual urgently needs professional ministration when he is troubled by *delusions* (a false belief that is not amenable to reason) such as being king of Cathay; or *hallucinations* (perceptions that do not exist) such as, "God spoke to me"; or *illusions* (an image or perception that does exist but is false as applied) such as, "The President wants me to come for a chat."

Other ways need to be found for coping with stresses. The very fact of *actively* (not passively) searching to mediate the psychological stress is partially ameliorative. The answer here is *act—don't just accept.*

Then, reflection on the actual cause of stress may go a long way toward its mitigation. If the stress is work related a change of jobs should be considered—if the individual has come to the clear decision that the stress is not easily tolerable. For example, are you distraught by jealousy that a coworker you don't like was promoted, or are you realistically assessing that yours is a dead-end job? In the latter event, consider how to make a change. The decision to make a change and the active consideration of how to make the change, rather than accepting a dead end will temper your stress. This is a form of coping.

Or, in a marriage in which bickering is stressful enough to be approaching the point of irritability (you should not have let it get so far anyway), try the unpredictable approach. Give praise and express a loving sentiment. The bickering may largely be due to lack of emotional support on the part of one spouse or both. He or she may think you are crazy. You may be, but you may also be right and wise. The wife of the pair may be hungering for a show of affection. Women as well as men need continued reassurance of love, especially if they are uncertain of themselves or of their own worth. A man needs reassurance that his spouse looks up to him, respects him, and above all clearly has confidence in him. Remember: *Don't react—act.*

One man, a patent attorney, was usually sent off to his office by his wife with an argument. The subject was always a renewal of an argument of the day before—continued unasked-for advice of how he should act with the children, complaints that his fees were too high (although she was able to live comfortably as a result of his fees), or recurring statements that their friends thought him obnoxious (which they denied). These were some examples of this wife's cheerful encouragement to her husband. He reasoned with her that in his work he had to be sharply alert and think of foreseeable and more especially, unforeseeable contingencies. Arguments were most stressful to him, and he pleaded with her to stop—but to no avail. *You cannot reason with emotions.*

But he was a creative person. One morning when he reached the office after the usual arguments, he telephoned his wife to reassure her of his affection, and lying grossly, told her how much he needed her. She answered with the usual calumny. But after three or four times, her attacks became milder, and within two weeks they ceased. He continued to give her reassurance; and a tolerable mode of living was established between them. While there was fundamentally something gravely wrong in their relationship that needed professional help, which neither of them wanted, they were able to continue with comparatively little damage to either. There was no emotional support to him, but active damage had ceased. Neither wanted to break up the marriage as apparently it served the purposes of both. Their neuroses fed each other's but in a tolerable fashion.

Similarly, a man under the guise of humor or good cheer usually kept a party going, sometimes in stitches, by using his wife as the object, the fall guy, of his jokes. She continued going to parties with him, though she was sure of being held up to ridicule, because she feared that what he would say in her absence would be much worse. At home he was silent—the stance of incommunicativeness of the "strong and silent" type. As a result of the stress of the continuous assailments to her self-esteem she developed a tic.

How to cope? At times it is necessary to sacrifice a relationship in order just to survive. A divorce was arranged. The tic disappeared shortly after the divorce.

In any relationship between two people there are three elements: (a) one person, (b) the other person, (c) the relationship. Stresses can creep in at any one of these parts. Psychological stresses are *intra*personal; social stresses are *inter*personal.

Often a *holding action* is necessary to *reflect, review,* and *reevaluate* a stress that is becoming destructive before taking a dramatic step. Action instead of reaction is the drug of choice, but action should not be precipitious. It can boomerang. It can produce a sense of loss if it causes a rupture, and added stress and depression often follow a sense of loss. For that reason the flu can be a most happy occasion. One can stay in bed at peace with one's Puritan conscience for such "idleness," which allows time and opportunity for three precious processes to take place: *reflection, review, and reevaluation.* There is, of course, a danger in that step: *an escape into illness,* often the manner of coping with stress. Productive or remedial? No! Destructive? Yes.

Another of the prime causes of stress is loss—separation from or loss of a loved person through death, or even loss of an object precious to a person. How does one cope with that, especially as it is often bound up with loss of hope—a serious development indeed.

The answer is *substitution.* Trying to forget is idle. Sweeping under the rug and suppressing grief or feelings about the loss is worse—it is reacting rather than acting.

Hence, in the event of a serious loss of a person, position, or object, *open up, talk it out, admit the loss,* and take quick steps to substitute. That is one reason why remarriage after the death of a spouse can be wisely considered provided that it is supportive of *both* parties; one-way streets do not run smoothly, and worse—they are exploitative.

For example, upon death of a spouse, after a good or even a stormy marriage, the dynamics in the family of survivors changes dramatically. It may bind the family more closely than it ever was before. But more often than not, an estrangement occurs between the children and the surviving spouse. This adds heavily to the burden of the surviving spouse. As a matter of survival he or she must act resolutely to prevent that additional stress from converting to distress in the form of emotional and physical discomfort or disease. It is truly a matter of survival, for slowly but inexorably survival is threatened.

The following is a case in point: The surviving spouse of one couple was the father. Relations between him and his children degenerated quickly after his wife's death, and at the end of two years the attitude of his two adult children toward him was not only a rejecting one but a conspicuously hostile one. He made no demands on his children except to make pleas for a civil relationship. "I want and need your love," he said to them, "but one cannot demand it as a tribute; it must come willingly from the gut. I love you both very much, but I do demand at least the civility you would extend to your neighbors or friends." The relationship continued to degenerate—the children talked to their father by long distance (they lived in different cities), but the conversations was at best nonemotive; at worst, imputations and accusations on the part of the children. The father realized that amelioration of his stress was critical, but he did not want to escape into a marriage as a matter of substitution.

But substitution was the answer to that untenable situation. *He substituted his feelings instead.* Slowly, painfully, but eventually successfully, he reduced his considerable emotional investment in his children. It did not change his way of life, as neither he nor his children depended on the other for financial support. The relation with his children became a tenable situation for him, with considerable reduction of stress, which enabled him to return to his professional activities. It became tenable for the children, too, as no emotional expenditures on their part were necessary. They now had a deplorable but successfully nonstressful relationship with the sociology and superficiality of a tea party.

In the folkways of the last generation, sending a girl on a sea voyage after an unhappy love affair was distinctly a mechanism of substitution. This was not a way "to forget" because there is sufficient time on a long sea voyage to recall and to mourn. But on a sea voyage there is an even greater opportunity for substitution by contact with other people.

In our culture we fear to sit still; reflection is considered idleness. But sitting still, periodically and recurrently, can be among your most precious of habits. *It is a stance productive of creativity.* You have to empty your mind of debris and drivel and a drive that becomes finally aimless. T. S. Eliot's *Ash Wednesday* speaks of it with utter simplicity and eloquence.

> Teach us to care and not to care
> Teach us to sit still.

It was previously mentioned that stress can manifest itself as illness. But it can also manifest itself emotionally as a lack of ease—emotional dis-ease; the transmutation into disease can be quick and deadly. And stress saps the psychic energy, which is an integral component of the creative juices.

How to turn stress into an asset? In the attempt to counter stress many events are reviewed. You do this with *reflection, review, and reevaluation*. Other dissatisfactions in your mode of living may then come to light. As the stress that stridently cried for attention is being guided to mitigation, the way to the relief to another problem—boredom— may come to the fore. And creativity may minister to that problem in living. In that way stress is turned into an asset, it can give one a greater awareness. But you must *act*, in order to gain its fruits.

How to avoid stress? It arises in living, in societal interaction, and in psychological intra-action. The principal objective is to recognize it and to act to ameliorate—you should not merely to accept it as a cross to bear. The remedies are more important, since prevention is not always possible.

Among the remedies—coping, adaptation, and particularly the 3 R's: reflection, review, and reevaluation. From that comes the 4th R: *revelation*. These are some of the ways of coping and adaptation or adjustment. The latter includes action toward changing the stressful conditions. But you must avoid precipitous action. Don't act hastily without using the three R's, or you may end up in perhaps a more stressful situation.

There is much more to stress. This chapter considers only highlights of the problem and some ways to manage stress in the interests of expanding creativity.

(See chapter 12, "Business and Loyalty" and chapter 19, "Time and Its Rhythm.")

WHAT TO DO. What should you do to defuse a stressful situation, assuming that you have already done the 3 R's—reflection, review, and re-evaluation?

1. *Tighten up on what's good.* Look at the positive and desirable aspects of what appears to be a stressful situation. For example, you have a job that is quite trying but the salary is good and, in fact, better than average. Then, (a) see if you are contributing to the stress; (b) how can you upgrade your performance, which may well reduce your stress if the stress comes from higher up.

2. *Loosen your hold on what is troublesome.* So often we accentuate our own stress by our expectations. For example, you have moved into a new community, in another state, because of a job transfer. Your new neighbors have not, or not yet, spread out the red rug to welcome you, had not even knocked at your door to invite you to coffee. It's their job to do so, you know. (It's similar to the convention of greeting: the person coming into the office says "good morning" first, not the ones who are already there.) So you have two alternatives, and if you think creatively you will have many more.

   Knock at your neighbor's doors—one day the neighbor at the left, the next day at the right. Say, "I'm your new neighbor, Jane Smith, and you're stuck with me. Please come in now for a cup of coffee—I also prepared some goodies with it." The neighbor will promise to come in—perhaps the next day—and she will, if for no other reason than to satisfy her curiosity. If she doesn't she will tell you her troubles—why she can't. So, you have already made a contact stick.

   If the neighbors ignore you despite your invitations, maybe you ought to reflect on why. Then, loosen your hold on what's troublesome. Instead, join your church, synagogue, PTA, cooking or garbage club or whatever. When other people start visiting your neighbors will soon take the initiative—you can be sure of that.

3. *Change what you can or accept what you cannot change.* But be sure that when you have decided that you cannot effect a change that you have *honestly* tried

and are not merely using it as a pretext for inactivity, passivity, or laziness.

For example, a very competitive and aggressive young man rose to the highest office in his professional association. But since he was not yet 35 years old, the by-laws prevented him from running for president, which he acutely wanted. And he was sure that he would be elected. But the three-year wait (he was 32) was a source of continuous stress to him. What do you do when you are so effectively blocked?

A simple and creative solution: you remove the blocks. Since he was sure that he would be elected, presumably friends and admirers were in the majority of the association. He got them to sign a petition to change the by-laws—rescinding the age requirement. He succeeded in getting a majority to sign the petition. And since he was an officer he also succeeded in having the petition acted upon, promptly. He ran for president and was elected.

4. *Love is for giving—not just for taking.* Perhaps a considerable component of your stress originates from your utter self-centeredness. That is, indeed, often the case. It is as if you are playing a broken record "No one has the troubles I have and the sun rises and sets in my navel but no one sees it."

No doubt you verbalize it differently, but if you have that feeling, use the 3R's—reflect, review, and reevaluate. You may discover that other people also exist. Then, involve yourself outside of yourself. You may actually learn something in the process, and many of your stresses will appear ephemeral and lessen.

Time and Its Rhythm

Each drummer marches to a different rhythm. The previous chapter devoted to stress briefly explored its relation to creativity. Stress can be transformed into distress and sap or pull down physical and emotional well-being. And a disturbance of the internal biological clock, which regulates biological rhythm, is a powerful stressor agent.

Virtually every natural event in connection with man and nature runs in rhythms or cycles, i.e., regular pause and recurrence at a predictable time. *But various functions have different cycles and march to a different rhythm.*

For example, menstruation occurs about every 28 days. The heart in man beats about 70 times a minute (about 35 times a minute in a horse and about 2,000 times a minute in a hummingbird). The moon observes a monthly cycle, which in turn influences the tides and numerous other events about which we are only recently beginning to learn. The sun is on a different cycle—one day. Man, too, is on a cycle of one day, which is called the circadian rhythm (*circa*—"about," *dies*—"day"). A human being's circadian physiological working is connected also with another phenomenon—light. Man is a daytime animal, his endocrine system is geared to activity during the day, which is called the diurnal rhythm. For example, the hormones of the adrenal gland begin to be secreted each day shortly before awakening and they peak during the late morning or early afternoon. They begin to decline in the afternoon and are the lowest in the midst of our sleep. Consonant with that, the temperature of the body is highest during activity and

156

lowest during sleep. The adrenal gland secretes many hormones concerned with activity, among other functions.

In fact, there is rhythmic fluctuation of the secretions of hormones in other glands. For example, the pituitary—the master gland of the body, the conductor of the whole endocrine or glandular symphony—is also dependent upon circadian rhythm.

There is another gland, the pineal (about one-half inch in size, buried deep in the brain next to the pituitary) which acts as one trigger to biological rhythm, or biorhythm. It converts light into a chemical messenger controlling secretion of hormones—the gonadotropins, involved with reproduction. It also is related to pigmentation because the pineal manufactures melatonin, which affects pigmentation. Light is thus a synchronizer of biological rhythm, or biological clocks.

Timing is integral in human affairs as well as internal functions. Oscillations are thus basic to life itself. These built-in biological clocks, monitoring biological rhythm or periodicity, control very practical functions in daily life. And there is more than one clock function in an organism. Each clock controls different functions in different organs at different times.

Where in the body is the biological clock (or clocks) housed? We don't know, however one external stimulus affects it and can disrupt it; that is an alteration of the light-dark cycle under which all living organisms live.

How widespread is the effect? Even the time at which one takes a medicine, not only the amount taken, can influence its action. For example, the timing between the very beginning of an infection—the bacterial invasion—and the administration of an antibiotic are of preeminent concern. At the instant that contamination or bacterial invasion takes place it is best to take medicine. Then the person's immunologic defenses are highest and an antibacterial agent can make them work under the optimum conditions—helping to kill of unwelcome bacteria when the body fights hardest to kill them off. A few hours later the body's defenses are fatigued, worn down, and do not energetically partake of the battle against invasion.

Another example: The effect of a medicine can be at times erratic, unpredictable, and quite different from that experience in the past. One of the reasons has to do with the biological rhythm or biorhythm. Since the secretion of various hormones or enzymes flucuates during the day or night, it may be due to interference with the normal metabolism of a drug. Such enzymes may interfere with utilization, thus weakening the effect of a drug, or they may suppress an inhibitor of a drug letting it work unrestrained or have a run-away action. A case in point are the liver enzymes. They may vitally affect the action of a drug at a certain time of the day, or night, but not at other times. In fact, this is a fertile and open field of investigation since as yet we know little about it. A whole new discipline, *chronobiology* (*chronos*—"time"), has recently been opened. The first laboratory of chronobiology has been formed at the University of Minnesota.

Mood shifts are also related to a biological rhythm. There is also a mood shift a few days before the symptoms of a cold appear. Many other physical and emotional events that occur are related to periodicity, or rhythm. The occurrence of jet lag—a stage of utter fatigue when traversing several time zones—is due to a disturbance of the biological rhythm. These living clocks of ours can be adjusted within a narrow range only, and in a limited way.

What makes biological clocks tick? Many of the unseen phenomena of the earth's geophysical fields are involved. They may not be cause or effect but merely associated phenomena. These living clocks, mysterious and mystical, are synchronized with the cosmos, for indeed every organism including plants, responds to them. Each of the organisms have their own rhythm and usually respond to several interrelated rhythms of different cycles of magnetic and cosmic influences.

Biorhythm is the practice of plotting on charts these invisible rhythms that are applicable to the individual for whom prepared. These rhythms, depending on an individual's birthdate, sketch out three cycles of 23, 28, and 33 days. The 23-day cycle charts the highs and lows of the physical state, the 28-day the emotional, and the 33-day

the intellectual highs and lows. They are figured and plotted often one or more years in advance. Is it a wonder then
that many large companies have the biorhythms of their
personnel plotted in order to enhance their efficiency and
to alert them to their *off-days* when they are more accident
prone?

While there is no indisputable evidence of the predictive
value of biorhythm charting of high and low days, there is
enough evidence of its validity beyond that of coincidence.
Biorhythm requires considerably more research, which indeed appears to be desirable and worthwhile.

Swissair reports that it has had no accidents since it has
decreed that if either pilot or copilot has critical (accident-
prone) days, he is not allowed to fly with another pilot or
copilot who also has a critical day. Since the Zurich Mu-
nicipal Transit Company has begun to advise its bus and
trolley-car drivers of their critical days their accident rate
has been reduced 50 percent.

Similarly, the Ohmi Railway Company of Japan had a
reduction of accident rate of 60 percent during the first
year's observance of biorhythms. After a few years there
was not one reported accident in 4 million kilometers by
bus and taxi drivers.

Companies other than those in transportation also find
that giving attention to biorhythms pays off. A number of
Japanese insurance companies prepare biorhythm charts
for their clients covered by accident insurance to increase
their awareness—hoping to reduce accidents.

How do biorhythms relate to creativity? Several ways:
biological rhythm is related to stress. Stress disturbs our
physical, mental, and emotional equilibrium until the coping mechanism is activated. The creative process may cause
an upheaval due to a shifting of attention, but it probably
does not bloom when an individual is in a state of stress.
And an upset of the biological rhythm, as say, during jet
lag, can be stressful. You don't think of creativity during jet
lag, you think of sleep. Practically, you don't know what to
think of, or what to do with yourself.

You no doubt know through their biographies, that some
highly creative people put themselves into stress to create.

That is a fable. For example, Ernest Hemingway was often drunk while writing. Dylan Thomas, is another example: He was virtually always drunk. And these were highly creative people. But they were creative *despite* their drunkenness and other stresses. Who knows how much more, or more easily, they would have been creative had they not been so frequently drunk?

In fact, *How It Was*, the biography of her husband by Mary Welch Hemingway quotes from a letter that Hemingway sent her when they were briefly separated. He told her that after having reduced his alcohol intake, he found that his work came much more easily and was much richer, and it pleased him greatly.

We all have our bad days—this is another way in which biological rhythm is related to creativity. If you attempt to go out of your deadly rut and soar into some creative endeavor on one of those down days and it doesn't work, don't despair. *It may not be your day.* Try again the next day, or the next, or the next week. You may well be surprised how easily one can soar when things are reasonably right and in rhythm.

CHAPTER 20

Boredom

Boredom sets your wheels going backward—it shifts your outlook to reverse. And it spins your wheels at the same time. Boredom is so widespread a phenomenon and at times so intensely and deeply upsetting that it could be called a national disease. The phrase "Age of Anxiety" has been applied to modern times when perhaps "Age of Boredom" is more appropriate.

What produces boredom? Many events, but some events are more powerful than others. And some states contribute to the cause of boredom, while others are the result of it.

The fundamental cause of boredom is an emotional emptiness—a lack of emotional resources. With this emptiness comes an inability to cope. There are various forms of coping mechanisms. One of the least constructive is withdrawal and depression, namely allowing yourself to be acted upon rather than acting. Being bored is also the reaction to monotony, dreariness, weariness of spirit, gloom and sadness, the feeling of futility. One loses interest in everything, is in effect bored.

These same responses also exist in depression. That is predictable because boredom leads to depression—the state where the zest for life has left an individual and an ennui or melancholy has taken its place.

Boredom is a giving up, a sinking down into dark thoughts and not even wanting to move out of them. Boredom is doing nothing about the monotony, the bedeviling void.

On a deeper level there is a loss of self-esteem. It is as if the silent question is put to oneself, "What am I good for?"—all part of the general picture of dissatisfaction with oneself. The longer one delays action, the more difficult it becomes to act because a paralysis of will, hence paralysis of action, overcomes you. One can be bored without showing the picture of lassitude and listlessness, which is the stage before depression. People can be frenetic and agitated, flailing about without concentrated aim, yet be bored and soon depressed. And one of the consequences or sequels of depression can be suicide.

Unremitting monotony, coupled with a lack of inner resources from which boredom arises, often precipitates the individual to antisocial acts in the attempt to cope with boredom. Think of the actions of Hell's Angels. Think of the youthful vandalism often visited on schools, houses of worship, or other public places. These acts are used by the emotionally sterile and emotionally crippled to work off energy.

What is the reason for boredom? There are many, depending on the social climate in which an individual finds himself. One of them is retirement. Retirement kills more people than work—when they have nothing to do and too much time in which to fill. This means that all of us should think about developing a consuming interest to practice an activity during our retirement that will stimulate us, fire our enthusiasm.

Paradoxically, our society's general affluence produces part of the framework in which boredom flourishes. When one has to scrounge for a livelihood one hasn't time to be bored; all time has to be energetically applied in order to survive. People who had to work long hours just to make a living had an aim and were continually busy working toward that aim—food, shelter, clothing; they had no time to be bored.

This does not mean that we need to return to a life of struggle or deprivation as a protection or cure for this modern disease. But from it one learns a royal remedy—*involvement*. Involvement as well replaces the sensory deprivation that also may produce boredom.

Today's societal mores include several litanies, talismans,

or catchwords. One of them is "don't get involved." This is a dreary comment on present-day alienation. Thomas Gordon, one of the putative prophets on behavior, has popularized another dogma: "Who owns the problem?" Meaning, "That's his problem, not my problem, so I will not be involved." This is an injunction to remain aloof, fenced with a specious justification for univolvement. Children, and adults too, are proud of staying cool, which means an abnegation of involvement.

The net result is *societal uninvolvement*, in which commitment becomes a dirty ten-letter word—more than twice as bad as a four-letter word. It becomes an unwillingness to enter the social matrix, or as the American philosopher Josiah Royce (1855–1916) eloquently described it, an unwillingness to enter "the blessed community of men."

It is only a matter of time before our uninvolvement is eventually and unmistakably converted from unwillingness to inability. The social feeling with its awareness and caring, its senses and sensations, is dulled if not snuffed out.

When this pattern of conduct, in which the aim is to turn away (don't get involved), is overlaid on individuals whose native resources have not been developed by social interaction, their emotional resources become further impoverished—become empty. Such individuals frenetically attempt to fill their void or their hunger for inner warmth with things. Moreover they want instant gratification, instant joy, right now, packaged in ready-made portions. Just heat and serve.

The urge is the puerile attempt to buy something, almost anything, to fill the void. Look at it in the framework of affluent retired people who buy things, take trips, yet come back as lonely and as bored as when they left. They are trying to fill a void with things, while the remedy lies in enriching inner resources by investing themselves in finding a consuming interest or passion.

Turning away from commitment means avoiding risks. If something is worth striving for, it is worth taking risk for. Every businessman, every student, every adult who is striving for something knows this. You will not lose anything, not even your boredom, if you don't take a risk. In the same way, you will not gain anything. When you turned away from a challenge, you have already lost.

Is there a remedy or a vaccine to protect you from boredom? Yes—creativity. But an activity that is done, say, for two hours on Sunday afternoon once in a while does not fill the bill.

The creative urge comes from the gut, one has to feel it, make a commitment to it. It can be evoked, or elicited, developed, magnified, then maximized and intensified, which converts it into a growth experience. When the thinking and feeling tracks are filled with stimuli there is no room for boredom. Metaphorically, when a given length of track is filled with railroad cars there is no more room for empty cars.

Work, involvement, or sheer activity are cures for boredom. But the work has to be more than busy work, more than counting paper clips. It has to be anything that an individual chooses provided that it enhulls him within itself—and the products of creativity are the answer. The issue is not *what thing* is produced, but the enthusiasm or consuming interest expended and expanded *in producing* the creative product or thing.

How to do it? How do you get the enthusiasm? By involvement, by curiosity, by trying your interest in a number of areas until the one area which you hit hits you and shrieks to you, EUREKA! That's what this book is all about. The other subjects are merely supportive to shed light on what helps or what hinders creativity.

Don't be a one-track mind at first—expand your horizons, enrich yourself in many areas until the oceanic feeling gets to you. Then you may well decide not to be a dilettante, you may want to zero in on one consuming interest.

How do other people try to handle those vast spaces of nothingness, of boredom? (Beware, too, some apply tiny Band-Aids.)

Some slump into the position of TV with beer. This is passive, stultifying, and aside from producing no growth, dulls the senses. It is like spectator sports that are passive and do not call forth participation, action, enrichment. Bellowing at a football game is not action, it is merely frenetic reaction.

Some people to escape boredom, especially in the cities with its abundance of bars or singles bars, drink themselves into oblivion. They fill up with alcohol, the number one drug-abuse problem in the U.S. After quaffing during the vacuous conversation at the bar they stumble home emotionally empty—and full of alcohol.

They attempt to cure their noninvolvement by conversation at the bar. If the objective is to find a one-night stand, at least that is a logical objective. But more than that the sum total is still disaffection with oneself, one's surroundings, with no substantive attempt to cure boredom by filling the void. Intelligent action by early involvement with life is necessary. The aim of alcohol and passivity is euphoria or oblivion, neither of which remedy the causes of boredom.

Affluence can also produce a means to attempt to cure this emptiness by flying into psychotherapy. Often professional advice is very much necessary. More often, it is an escape into narcissism, and a desperate attempt to "know who I am" or some such psychological cliché. More often, therapy forms a subject of conversation for people who have nothing more to say than to discuss their respective shrinks. It can be a conversation piece, some object, like a coffee table.

What to do toward a remedy for boredom? Aside from the means discussed above, bear these points in mind.

(1) Don't program your children for boredom and its decadence by gratifying their every wish; let them learn deferred gratification. (Instant gratification is what a helpless infant needs.) Let them work for what they want. Parents are tempted to give children all those things the parents were deprived of during their own youth. But while you may have been deprived of things, you actually became enriched, for you learned that deferred gratification can be productive. If that were not so, ironically you probably could not afford the things that you so eagerly wish to give your clamoring children.

(2) There is nothing static in life. If you don't grow, you shrink. And if you have shrunk even a shrink cannot make you grow. We grow by our own efforts.

(3) Become involved with people and in something that appears to you to be worthwhile. It will increase your sense of worth as a person, increase your level of functioning and self-acceptance, rather than making you feel like an inanimate providing machine.

(4) Look and plan ahead. Bored people do not look ahead. It will help you increase your tolerance for ambiguity, for uncertainty. Examine your aims. How often have the attempts at euphoria or oblivion paid off? There are more enduringly satisfying alternatives.

(5) Above all do not let boredom cover your sense of humor, which can give you perspective and which is an eminently successful remedy for boredom. When we have lost the ability to laugh at ourselves we have truly lost.

When you *feel good* you'll *feel well*.

And when you *feel good* you may well *do good* to those around you, if for no other reason than in the interests of intelligent selfishness. And you will be *involved*. Involvement is a critical step to replace the monotony of the lonely, isolated space around you. This emptiness is the soil in which boredom grows and flourishes.

(*See* Appendix: "What Are We Living For" and "What Does One Do For Fun?")

Boredom is a state no one gives you; you give it to yourself—it's up to you. But remember, involved people are too fulfilled to be bored.

CHAPTER 21

Fatigue

How many people are there who complain of persistent fatigue! How many who say they are tired all the time?

At some time or other all of us feel fatigued, but for a short time. Fatigue is normal after physical exertion or strenuous exercise, but then the tired feeling passes after a brief rest or overnight sleep.

But persistent fatigue, especially on awakening in the morning, is also a concomitant of boredom. Frequently they come together as an unholy pair—fatigue is often caused by boredom, and boredom causes fatigue. There are no antiboredom pills against that fatigue.

Naturally while persistent fatigue is a frequent result of boredom, it does not mean that boredom is the only cause of mental or physical weariness. There are other causes of fatigue that should also be considered so that we can eliminate them from our lives.

Some reasons are medical. An underactive thyroid will cause fatigue. Another frequent medical cause is fatigue following an illness that saps energy, such as an infection. Consider the well-known fatigue after a bout with the flu. Fatigue also follows an operation or childbirth. And after mononucleosis, fatigue in an otherwise previously active and energetic person may continue for weeks. But if you feel fatigued, especially if you do not have a medical history of fatigue, see a smart doctor.

Another important cause for fatigue is situational, relating to your situation—your job, your marriage, your self-acceptance. Is your job a chore? Is your marriage corrosive? How do you look upon yourself or your status?

You may be sick and tired (note the word, *tired*) of any of them. And the chronic situation makes you tired and fatigued just to think of them. It is the emotional stress that wears one down and weakens one by prolonged pressure.

Perhaps most of the situational collisions causing fatigue lie in a marital or familial situation. Even if your job is the predominant cause of your fatigue, if you have emotional support from your spouse it makes it easier to bear the drain caused by your job because you have hope; you think of home as a haven, a hermitage, a place of surcease with a loving partner. And with a show of confidence and emotional nourishment, a smart, sensitive spouse raises your self-esteem, hence your self-acceptance.

But if your fatigue arises largely from a continuously contentious marital relationship, an on-going confrontation, the fatigue not only will continue but also will be exaggerated and deepened. And that alone produces other dissatisfactions that feed the fatigue response, becoming neverendingly the serpent biting its own tail.

For example, a marriage may be an ordeal for one partner. But it may be actually distressful to the other partner. There is no one-way street in marriage. A tumultuous relationship gives no satisfactions to either party even though one may be a warrior-spouse and the other reacts with the insidious acts that a guerrilla-spouse uses in his or her own defense, with provoking actions. *It is rarely the fault of one mate,* usually it is the clash that grows out of a skirmish to win a battle—a strong bid for power, dominance, or ego fodder on the part of one spouse. We are not speaking here of the occasional marital disagreement that normally occur on specific points, but of a full-scale operation of hostility engaged in by both combatants. Both parties are belligerents, with occasional short truces not for peace but to regroup energies for a new campaign.

The battle is fought most fiercely in bed, no matter what the precepitating or proximate cause may appear to be.

When a marriage is on the rocks the rocks are in bed.

And the rocks bruise both partners. The wife may feign

fatigue—"I-gotta-splitting-headache." The husband is possibly relieved that he does not have to perform, he too is chronically fatigued and soon he loses even his interest in sex. The marriage itself is fatigued and fatiguing. You cannot make love to a partner you don't like, except perhaps on a one-night stand. When the sex drive is lowered or even temporarily lost, the marriage is lost, though the partners may live together for a variety of circumstances and reasons. They may even be compatible roommates.

Before you blame your partner, ask yourself these questions—and don't answer yourself flippantly. Can you love and show love to another person? And as important: Can you *accept* love and show your pleasure at doing so? Or, do you love only yourself—with abandon and to a degree that *you should* show your sponse? This may hold the key to a situational fatigue.

Naturally, if you lose a love relationship your incentive in involvement outside of yourself can be severely disturbed. You may become sick-of-the-world fatigued. You don't feel like taking on the simple daily problems that suddenly grow in your mind gigantic size. It justifies in your mind your doing nothing—a bone-wrenching fatigue has set in.

Such deep interpersonal troubles, or even a continuous succession of little vexations, can tire us out, or depending on our tolerance, fatigue us, often profoundly. When fatigued, emotionally and mentally, we cannot handle let alone solve problems. We cannot even assess how a change of some circumstances can get us to convert our wretchedness into reasonable satisfaction. Conflict is then not the cause of the passivity. Fatigue produced by conflict is the enemy.

We have discussed fatigue, as arising from unfortunate happenings which assail a person. But fatigue may often be the result of an embarrassment of riches. An example may be the person who has no unsatisfied needs but gets bored. He lives on the superficial skin of life. Again, boredom breeds fatigue, then profound depression.

The reason we discuss fatigue is that it is related to boredom which creativity can mitigate, or help us overcome.

Many a couple in the middle- or upper-middle-class stratum with education and accomplishments do get bored, perhaps fatigued. This happens to them because their involvement is totally outside of themselves as a couple and because their inner resources are very sparse. The man may be in business or in one of the professions. The wife may be a career woman thoroughly involved outside of herself during the day in her work. They meet at home after the workday. They discuss the day's events at dinner, and after dinner they have nothing left to say to each other since they do not or cannot communicate as people. During the ritual TV watching they get fatigued, hastened by overeating and depression produced by alcohol. They are bored to death.

Creativity comes in as an antidote or protective against boredom—as discussed in many places in this book. Boredom and fatigue are related, and are distressing to the spirit if there is any spirit left. *And tedium* is an affliction not easily cured. It is more easily prevented by enriching one's spirit. The alternative is boredom or a raging disquiet. The life of the spirit is put into a continuous dissonance. But it can be converted into a harmony with our inner selves by devotion to our creative potential to which we respond or to something outside of our little field of vision. The opposite of responsiveness is insensitivity—and further disaffection. But accentuate the positive and find some gifts in the other person, and you'll find your soul will speak out and your spirit will soar.

(*See* Appendix, "What Are We Living For" and "What Does One Do For Fun.")

CHAPTER 22

Insight, Intuition, Intelligence

The previous chapter tells one how to get out of the boredom swamp—and what *not* to do. This chapter is devoted to the very heart of creativity. It deals with what you *can* do, and is intended to describe why insight and intuition are vital to your creativity.

Since no one really knows what intuition or insight is, definitions would be a specious exercise. You cannot define the unknown, but you can describe it. You can know it by its effect, or you can recognize it by hindsight. And that hindsight enriches your perception to use it in future events. But, more particularly, you can use it only if you can recognize it.

Both intuition and insight are phenomena of inner space. The mysterious events that take place in our minds, which are ordinarily covered by a curtain of fog or forgetfulness or repression, at times illuminate and in their incandescence can precipitate a feeling as to what we might do in the future. You get a hunch—that, broadly speaking, is intuition. At other times the curtain of fog parts enough to give you an inner view that converts sight to insight. *Insight is the wisdom of the soul.*

How do you get intuition? You don't simply get it. You have it. You only need to relax to welcome it. Don't work hard at forcing it—just don't suppress a hunch when it comes to you. You will become more comfortable with an intuition and you will more readily recongize it and be able to act on it if you let it happen. An inductive leap created by a hunch or intuition can skip over many steps. Intuition allows you to get from square one to square six without the laborious hopping through the intervening squares.

The first step toward enriching your intuition is to *trust it,* even though at first you find it does not serve you well. Highly creative people all depend on their intuition, it gives them the insight toward their discoveries. Great examples of creativity which do not necessarily mean paintings or scientific discoveries but can be as simple as a new mode of life, have rarely come through hard conscious thinking. They have been perfected by conscious application or refinement of an image. But the image itself comes in a simple childlike way—following a hunch.

Intuition tells you where to look. It has an unerring homing instinct for truth. Intuition guides your working on an unconscious level, guiding and sparking your imagination. The important thing is to welcome these hunches, to be relaxed and receive them—they are messages from your unconscious.

Following hunches can pay tremendous dividends, even in such "scientific" activities as making diagnoses. Listening to his unconscious, a physician one day cancelled his afternoon hours in order to make a house call on a little girl who lived some distance away. Her mother was in no hurry but telephoned him only to tell him of her daughter's fever and slight nausea. While the symptoms were not extraordinary, it turned out that the little girl had a serious type of meningitis. He hospitalized her none too soon and thereby saved her life.

What was the intuitive leap that made him take that step? He merely had asked the mother what her daughter was doing and she said, "Nothing, she is just lying in bed and looking up at the ceiling." The word "ceiling" triggered something buried deep in the doctor's unconscious, and he acted on it. Only after the fact did he realize that a feverish child lying quietly instead of restlessly might have a stiff neck—meningitis.

That doctor also described several other instances where a hunch had saved a patient's life. One instance was that of a nine-month-old infant. His intuition told him that the infant had appendicitis. Two surgeons refused to operate because appendicitis in such a young infant is almost unheard of, but more particularly, the baby's abdomen was soft, had no masses or spasm—signs that nearly always accompany appendicitis. When the doctor finally prevailed upon a third surgeon to operate, it was none too soon. A pus-filled appendix was removed.

To what did the doctor ascribe his hunch? He did not know. *But he always followed his hunches, he said, even if they were contrary to logic.* He had faith in his intuition. His faith was strengthened by previous incidents.

Another time he had a hunch about a young patient that was so remote he did not heed it. It was something he couldn't point his finger to, and moreover the specialists he consulted advised him against doing anything. He was much disquieted. He just knew something was wrong, but he didn't know what. Weeks later the young patient developed rheumatic fever—a sad occurrence. It is helpful to continuously test our intuitions.

Rarely have truly exceptional ideas come through conscious thinking. If you are in the habit of putting everything that comes to mind in little watertight compartments you will be losing the precious quality of insight. A stereotype kills new visions or creativeness. A rigid ordering of thoughts turns off creative ideas. Keep your visions in bold strokes—details at the beginning will drown you in trivia. You may need them later to test out your creative ideas, but you will not get any creative ideas by zeroing in on details at the beginning.

Allow yourself to dare to imagine. This will give you a different coherence of ideas and disclose new perspectives. And creativity also means seeing how relationships dovetail, how nonverbal cognition of relationships forms new images. Intuition leads to insight leads to creativity.

That is the reason you should not discard ideas, half-baked though they may seem to be at first. The ideas that come to you in the stage of being half-awake, half-asleep are often the most promising. They may bring to your conscious mind analogies from other fields—a sort of unconventional nonconformity, nonstereotypical thinking—which also leads to creativity.

Don't be held back in allowing your intuition, hence your creativity, from expressing itself from the fear that you have no originality. Everyone has that quality. Most plays, stories, ideas are rarely original, that is, in the sense that the theme was thought of before. There is nothing really new under the sun. It is the application of an old idea, the placing of it in a new setting, a new insight into an old problem that is the heart of the subject of most creative ideas.

But originality per se is not a virtue. The important thing is how you apply it, how you present an idea that makes the difference. And that is a creative endeavor often triggered by intuition.

Carl Jung drew a graphic-verbal map of this area: "Awareness and creativity are not rationally but intuitively conceived—through dreams, visions, reflections—in fact, going into the cistern of the unconscious."

Insight is found in unexpected places. In 1922 Henry Luce saw an advertisement for tires in the New York City subway that read: "Time to Retire." "Time" was a natural for the name of a magazine that he and Briton Hadden had been talking about starting for two years previously. What is more natural than the name *Time* for a magazine of timely happenings?

People not as open to a creative blast may merely respond with a yawn to the word "retire," but humor is also a creative endeavor. Surely one should not attempt to explain jokes by a footnote. But in considering the guts of humor, there comes to mind that the subject of humor is often an ordinary occurrence transferred into an unusual situation. For example, a man coming home unexpectedly found his wife in bed with the family doctor. Flustered, the wife said that the doctor was taking her temperature. Thereupon the husband, apologizing for his suspicion and thanking him for making a house call, said to the doctor: "When you take out the thermometer and it doesn't have numbers on it, I won't pay your bill for this house call."

Another example of an ordinary occurrence transferred

into an unusual situation is the ancient joke about the patient who fights a nurse who has been ordered to give him an enema. She finally persuades him to cooperate. After administering the enema she asks: "Now, that wasn't so bad was it. Not much more than having a cup of tea." The patient grunted, "It was O.K., but . . ." "But what," asked the nurse. "It was O.K., but it was too sweet."

CHAPTER 23

Decision, Judgment, and Perception

You may be asking yourself, What purposes do intuition and insight serve? How can I put them to use enriching my creative potential? Can they also be used in the activities of daily life?

On the whole, there are only a few things we can be positive about. But in this instance one can answer the above questions enthusiastically! Indeed, intuition and insight augment creativity, and both figure in and heighten the activities of daily life.

Why? And how?

First the why. We are continually faced with the need to form judgments on which we then base our *decisions*. And decisions figure in all our activities, though some are so minor (such as, what to order in a restaurant) that we do not dignify them by the name of decision. And conversely, too, judgments are one of the actions that are based on decisions—after a decision is made.

It is not easy to form a judgment—a great number of elements enter into it. Our intuitions, vibes or hunches are often invaluable influences which we can use to make wise decisions. The worst problem is that we can not be sure in advance of the results of an action that follows our judgment. The faculty of prophecy is not given to finite man. But we can base our decisions partially on what we have learned; partially on the experience of other people; partially on our examinations of the alternatives, and by reflection on the relative weights of the alternatives; partially on logic, although some people unfortunately often base themselves wholly on it.

But many a decision can well be based on the indefinable and intangible quality called intuition and can often materialize into a wise decision.

If you have ever been involved in the policy-making echelon of a business or any other large organization you will recall how incredibly indecisive many heads are. And at times they vacillate even after having painfully made a decision by rescinding it, and reconsidering alternatives they have previously rejected, often several times.

Indecision is not solely a problem with the businessman, in fact he is more likely to make a reasonably prompt decision, though it may not be the best one. But indecision cuts across many disciplines, even with academic people. A scholastic of the nineteenth century named Borodin theorized on decisions and came up with the theorem of Borodin's Ass. That hypothesis states that a donkey standing exactly in the middle of two piles of hay will starve to death because it will not be able to decide which pile to begin eating. Apparently the donkey in the experiment was more decisive than the scholar, it ate the left pile first and then began to eat the right pile. Some donkeys, it is said, are smart people.

Some people, fully confident of the dependability of their intuitive nature, virtually base their judgments and decisions wholly on intuition. But if this is new territory for you, don't do this until you have become accustomed to it, feel comfortable in it, and particularly have been able to gain a reasonable track record in the use of intuition. Eventually, when intuition vouchsafes you an insight, you will depend on it for a self-correcting factor in your judgment. For example, if your intuition tells you to climb to the top of the Washington Monument with a gallon can of tomato juice, it is not intuition. It is the need to see a psychiatrist.

Until then there are several steps to remember in forming judgments. The more changes there are in your environment, the greater the number of judgments and decisions you will have to make in order to cope with change.

Here are some tips toward making sound judgments.

(1) Get the facts first—even if you will depend on your intuition to form judgments and decisions.

(2) Consider the possible consequences of the alternatives open to you. Only after weighing them should you form your judgment.

(3) Given the same facts, a wise decision often depends on the framework in which it is to be exercised. For example, it may appear wise to change a given job; but at a time of increasing unemployment the picture may change.

(4) Don't delude yourself that a given decision you have to make or judgment you have to form must be consistent with what you have done before. *Consistency for its own sake is no virtue.* It may be a euphonious term for rigidity.

(5) Like consistency, objectivity is also praised as a virtue. But we often delude ourselves that we are objective, and we seldom are wholly objective. Unconsciously, we usually see what we want to see. And perhaps full objectivity, if it is possible, is not an undiluted virtue, it may well take no heed of compassion or even of justice. Also, avoid being taken in by so-called "scientific judgment." There is no science in judgment because no judgment is fully free from emotion. The only valid scientific judgment is in scientific work itself.

After arriving at a position, do play devil's advocate to yourself. Consider the probable effects of an opposite position from the one you've taken. It may strengthen your stand—or modify it. There are few black-and-white situations.

(6) When arriving at a position by patterning yourself on a previous incident, step back and ask yourself: Is the present position a correspondent or a contradistinctive one when compared with the previous incident? The result may surprise you. You may possibly find that the present situation corresponds to the previous incident only on the surface in an unimportant way, while the crux of both incidents is basically different.

(7) While contemplation and reflection before forming judgments and coming to a decision are valuable, taking an unduly long time in forming judgment is not necessarily the

best method. It may be a matter of your customary indecisiveness. Often with intuition the quick or instant decision turns out to be the correct one. But usually in the long run the course that is worse than a wrong decision is no decision at all. And if you think that by not making a decision you avoid one, think again—failure to decide is also a decision.

An absurd example of the latter is the true story of an editor of a national magazine. As is well known, news media aim to be first to carry articles about almost anything *new*—novelty being much sought for. When Transcendental Meditation first came upon the scene in the U.S., a writer proposed doing an exclusive article on it, then considered a mind-blowing development. The editor-in-chief whom he approached hesitated, as he was not sure *how many people had heard of TM* ®, completely ignoring the idea that especially if they had not they would first read about it in his magazine! This would be a feather in any editor's cap. He wanted "to think it over" for a few weeks! The writer sold the article to a competing magazine and it appeared a few weeks later, leaving the first editor to explain his own editorial myopia to his publisher.

(8) Consult the sages. But you cannot do it just before you need to make a decision. You consult them through a lifetime of reading and reflecting. In that way you are a living witness to thousands of incidents in the stories and situations you have read about. How would you have acted in place of a given character in a book? A constant dialogue with the author of what you read helps you to multiply your experiences and sharpen your acuity. In a riskless way you get practice making judgments and decisions. *Never make a decision when angry.*

(9) A judgment or decision is based on discrimination or choice between two or more options. It is at this point that your sense of values or your value system integrally enters a judgment or decision. (This is another reason why the idea of objective judgment is froth and fluff—a myth.) Decisions are not always easy to make, but they become much simpler and wiser if you consider the aim or basis on which you want to make them. Is it your aim to make a just

or a self-serving decision? Answer yourself honestly. Would you rather make one that is compassionate or just? After you answer that to yourself, put yourself in the place of the other person and ask yourself again. *No decision can be right or wrong unless you have honestly tested it against your value system*—if you aim to be honest with yourself.

The above are some of the aspects to be considered in forming a judgment and making a decision. Unfortunately, it is not possible to give an unfailing set of directions toward making only the "right" decisions similar to directions for making a cup of instant coffee.

The reason that decision-making has been considered is to point out that creativity can help you tremendously in forming adequate judgments and wise decisions. These are often augmented, intensified, or magnified by taking other than the "tried-and-true" steps. For example, the solution ascribed to King Solomon in judging which of the two women who claimed a given child is the real mother was a flash of genius or a rare stroke of intuition. He certainly did not use the "market research approach" of how to determine who is the true mother.

You have heard the expression, "Don't stand there—do something!" when a decision is desired or long in coming. In my opinion the demand itself is fallacious. What is desired is a *wise* action, not merely action for its own sake.

For example, the new chairman of the U.S. Consumer Product Safety Division said he hoped to "make a difference." (He did not say that the difference would be an improvement.) In addition he stated in his reorganization address, "You may not agree with all of our actions, but I can assure you that there will be action." The listener could not be encouraged that the action would be one that would improve the functions of the agency, since the inference was just action. Would the action make the function of the agency better? You can understand what you want by that statement.

Often we learn affirmatively by negative examples. Also, it's not a sin to fail. Negative examples often throw a sharp picture on the screen, of what not to do and conversely, they give us a better focus on what to do. To illustrate, here are some examples of utter stupidity or miserable judgment.

(1) On the bulkhead separating first class from coach in one of the first jet airplanes a beautiful mural had been painted. It was the picture of a handsome Greek youth with wings. A Greek youth with wings? It was reminiscent of Icarus who flew too close to the sun, which melted his artificial wings, causing him to fall into the Aegean Sea and drown. This would have been a splendid decoration almost anywhere. But on an airplane? Wings that failed? A drowning in the sea?

(2) A young woman won a regional beauty contest and rode on the hood of a car in a parade celebrating the event. It was hot on the hood. At the end of the parade the skin or her buttocks had been burned off, requiring plastic surgery for repair. Why didn't she get off when she felt it become insufferably hot? She said: "I wanted maximum exposure."

(3) A man took oral contraceptives for six years. During that time his wife had five children. Didn't it occur to him that something was radically wrong, surely after the second pregnancy? "No," he said, "I followed directions, and it didn't say I should not take the pills."

(4) A publisher of a prominent chain of newspapers in the Midwest wrote a scathing editorial that ran in one of his papers, the flagship of his media empire, excoriating a political candidate who was running for elected office. The publisher ordered it run despite the fact that the paper had long editorially supported that candidate. When asked the reason for his extraordinary behavior particularly since the morale of the paper's employees had sunk low, he said that he had nothing against the candidate, that he even liked him both personally and politically. He had written the editorial merely to show his independence and to increase the image of credibility of his paper!

(5) Publishers very rarely accept for consideration manuscripts when they come in "over the transom" (trade term for an unsolicited manuscript). Unless they solicit a manu-

script from a writer, they usually accept manuscripts only through literary agents. Yet, a manuscript received from a literary agent often gets its first reading by a reader at the lowest and most inexperienced end of the totem pole. These readers, green in experience, who know little about the adequacy or marketability of a book, in effect make the final decision when they reject a manuscript out-of-hand, for in that case, it is not further reviewed.

(6) Political candidates openly speak of *campaign strategy*. Strategy is anything but a forthright and honest approach—*strategy degenerates into manipulation*. But no harm comes from that because the connotation of that danger clearly goes over the heads of the voters. *No one brings up the point that strategy is manipulative of people's minds.*

(7) People try too hard to understand what may be left unspoken in the minds of opponents or other people with whom they interact by wondering, *"What do they mean by that?"* But while trying to determine what is under the surface, they ignore the other person's body language, a valuable indicator of what people really mean. To test how body language speaks, put on a TV program and turn off the sound. You will probably have an idea of what the actors and actresses are saying, even without reading their lips. Then to test yourself and your perceptions turn on the sound.

(8) Government is by far the largest corporation in the country. It inveighs against big government yet continues to swell itself more and more with often unnecessary personnel. If the intention is to create a permanent WPA it would be sensible.

(9) Government spends many millions of dollars on civil preparedness, a laudable aim. But the plans for distribution and accessibility of supplies in the event of a nuclear explosion are so poor and thoughtless that fatally injured civilians will not even have the solace of drugs to relieve their pain before they die—attention will be given to those who are less injured and have a chance to pull through. This is the principle of *triage*—choosing who will live and who will die—for there will not be enough supplies to serve both the injured and the dying.

(10) Many hospitals are so named that they inspire dread in patients rather than hope. As illustrations: *Home for Incurables; Jewish Chronic Disease Hospital; Hospital for Ruptured and Crippled* (since renamed Hospital for Special Surgery); *Crippled Children's Center; Hospital for Sick Children* (somewhat idiotic as there is no need for a Hospital for Well Children.) This labeling may, however, be done intentionally with forethought. Such gravely named institutions tug more effectively on the heartstrings of potential donors.

If you would like to revel in a book devoted to human stupidity—for the negative examples that it carries—see the reading list for Paul Tabori's *The Natural History of Stupidity*.

An excellent example of judgment in cutting through the red tape that is characteristic of government is exemplified by what happened to the following ruling promulgated during the dark days of World War II:

Such preparations shall be made as will completely obscure all Federal buildings occupied by the Federal Government during an air raid for any period of time from visibility by reason of internal or external illumination. Such obscuration may be obtained either by blackout construction or by terminating illumination.

Franklin D. Roosevelt, in addition to the weight of decisions during the war, rewrote the above sentence as follows: "Cover the windows and turn off the lights."

In common speech, an individual with poor judgment is called a fool though, of course, he pridefully and blindly believes he is wise. Good judgment is a matter of putting sense together with intuition and insight—and this is where creativity comes in.

CHAPTER 24

Memory and its Traces

The phrase *learn by experience* would be empty were it not for the faculty of remembering. Memory enables us to retain a recollection to add to the sum total of our fund of information, sensations, reactions. Thus, all our activities are strongly related to memory, an integral component of everything we do.

Judgment is in great measure related to memory because our current judgments and decisions depend greatly on our recollection of past events and experiences. Were it not for the facility of memory that we all have, learning would be pointless. We must learn and retain at least a fraction of what we have learned in order to apply it.

People often have an imperfect and unrealistic expectation of memory. They feel that one either has a good memory or one does not. This is simply not so because memory is actually not lost (except in brain damage) but merely covered over. And it *can* be improved. But even though memory is largely a psychological process, there are important physiological factors involved. Impairment can occur though straight physical factors, as for example, the memory loss due to arteriosclerosis (degenerative changes in the blood vessels of the brain), or the development of a plaque containing amyloid due to aging.

In aging, memory, especially of recent events, drops off steeply. The phenomenon of an aged person remembering clearly details that may have occurred fifty years ago but not remembering those of a day or two ago is well known. The loss of memory in alcoholics or heavy drinkers is well

184

known. Alcohol is a protoplasmic poison and especially affects brain and liver cells. Electroshock or electroconvulsive therapy (ECT) given in the treatment for depression obliterates memory for a time. Brain damage as well as alcoholism can produce loss of memory.

But our principal interest in this area is (a) how can we intensify or improve our memory and its recall; and (b) how may we use memory as a tool in the creative process? *Both are possible*. Remember that you never lose the memory of something you learn. The problem lies in retrieving it—and you can block yourself by anxiety, by fearing that you cannot recall something, or by trying too hard. *Work smart, not hard*.

STEPS TO IMPROVE YOUR MEMORY

(1) Make sure you understand thoroughly the topic or the event that you want to remember. Then repeat or review, saying out loud or even to yourself what you have just learned. For example, to remember the name of a person to whom you have just been introduced, do not merely mouth the perfunctory, "How do you do." Instead state his or her name with your greeting. And refer to them by name again when you speak to them. The moral here is: *understanding and repetition*.

(2) To remember what you just learned, associate it with something, with more than one item if possible. You can remember anything if you are sure to associate it with something you know. Similarly, you can spell tricky words accurately by association. For example, is it spelled "receive" or "recieve?" Think *Adam not Eve*—and you will find that your association is sound because the last three letters of the latter word spell Eve, and you are supposed to think *Adam not Eve*. So the right spelling is the former word—"receive." You can make your own mnemonics easily.

Also, associate an abstract idea with something concrete. For example, unless you are a theologian, you will rarely use the word *antinomian*. Would you like to remember what it means? It is a concept that faith alone (not the moral law) is necessary to salvation. Remember the phrase: The name of the game is faith. The internal rhyme (name-game) is also an aid to memory. Also, how often have you thought of a long-forgotten joke, because you were reminded of it by a similar joke you just heard. How many times have *you* used the phrase "that-reminds-me"?

The greater the number of *hooks* you have on which to hang things the more likely you will remember, even if one or two hooks do not help you retrieve. For example, if you wish to remember a telephone number, figure out from the dial what it spells, such as, 487-2263 spells "husband." The number 564-6766 spells "Johnson." Other numbers, like 369-3672 are easy as there is a progression of 3's—3-6-9; the remainder is 3 dozen (36) and 6 dozen (72). The point: *Use redundancy and association to help you remember.*

(3) Think in terms of units. When setting a table you need only remember a unit—fork-knife-spoon—and need never worry about forgetting any one of them when you think of a unit. The point: *Think in terms of groups, of relationships.*

(4) *Use mnemonics with some meaning.* Mnemonics are devices to help you remember a situation. For example, who remembers the number of days that each month has? We have more important things to remember. But once as a child you learned the rhyme you will never forget:

> Thirty days hath September
> April, June and November
> All the rest have thirty-one
> Excepting February alone,
> To which we twenty-eight assign
> Till leap year give us twenty-nine.

As a matter of fact, the reason we more easily remember a street that has a *name* rather than a number is because a name has a meaning, even if we do not know the person for whom it was named.

Another mnemonic will help you to determine if a given

word you want to use is spelled princi*pal* or princi*ple*. Remember that a principal is a person—a *pal*. Concepts, ideas, doctrines, which are principles, are not people (except that we hope that more principals would have principles).

We are changing over to the metric system of measurements. Do you know if dekagram is 10 grams or 1/10 of a gram? And what about decigram? They both trigger the numeral 10. The key is the mnemonic *GILD*. It makes you remember that *G*reek *i*ncreases and *L*atin *d*ecreases. Thus *deka*, which is Greek, is 10 grams but *deci* which is Latin is 1/10 of a gram.

How does a student remember the 12 cranial nerves? Simple—if you use the nonsensical mnemonic: *On old Olympus' towering top, a fat-assed German viewed a hop.* The first letter of each word suggests the following: olfactory, optic, oculomotor, trochlear, trigeminal, abducens, facial, acoustic, glossopharyngeal, vagus, accessory, hypoglossal—which are the 12 nerves which originate in the brain and are distributed through the face and neck. How else could one remember them with relative ease?

Do you move the clock ahead in the spring for Daylight Saving Time, or do you move it back? Easy to remember the mnemonic, *spring ahead*. It means that you spring (jump, move) ahead in the spring. Set the clock in the spring an hour ahead. And in the autumn—*fall back*. Set clocks back an hour.

(5) Summary:

(a.) Relax—work smart, not hard.

(b.) Learn and be sure you understand what you have learned.

(c.) Repeat to fix it in your memory.

(d.) Associate what you have learned with something else you know, as association is one of the vital steps in remembering. Observe details, use hooks, use redundancy.

(e.) Think in terms of group or units or relationships.

(f.) Use mnemonics—aids to memory—form pictures in your mind. It is obvious that to remember you should have an interest or motivation in doing so. Observe details, fix them in a total picture. The more hooks you have the more persistent the memory.

The objective of this book is to magnify, expand, and heighten creativity. Memory is only a well from which to draw experiences, feelings, etc., the raw material of creativity. This part of the chapter has only a sketchy outline on memory. To go into in greater depths, see the reading list at the end of the book.

How to use memory.

Ambiguity: In function the brain has built into it certain ambiguities—anatomically and electrophysiologically. *From this ambiguity originate many creative products or events.* Because our thinking or communication or understanding or perceptions are frequently skewed, as wires often cross and some input of our understanding is short-circuited, certain aberrant behavior or ideas spring from it. It does not mean that you have to be crazy to be creative—in fact, creativity requires an over-all healthy framework. But these aberrant perceptions are taken by the creative person and transformed into creative products.

For example, think of the aberrant drug-induced impressions that Coleridge transformed into the incredibly beautiful poem, "Kubla Khan."

Or take the unorthodox idea of a three-legged stool, which is as steady as the classical four-legged one but is perfect for small spaces and is more easily collapsible and portable. It is said to have originated in a dream where the dreamer was forced to redistribute these legs as *one leg was missing.*

Where there is ambiguity there is an opportunity for creativity because ambiguity admits of *more than one way of looking at a situation.*

Dreams: An almost inexhaustible source of creative ideas resides in dreams. In dreaming you let yourself go and roam in places you would not often dare to go in a waking state. You see scenes of unearthly splendor; magnificence beyond imagination; radiance of an unearthly light illuminating scenes of pageantry glittering with blazes of glory in the air you breathe in with every breath.

Then unwillingly you wake up. Wouldn't you like to remember the dream, even a fraction of it?

Or you dream of an oppressive churlishness in the air, a splenetic aura that chills your bones. Even the inanimate scenery is sullen, sneering, and snarling. But it is not inanimate—the trees begin to move with legs—and advance! There is consternation! You become a huge panic button. You cannot move, the swirling creatures are wearing your legs and are waving arms, your arms, which have multiplied on the branches. You are powerless, but at least you can quiver and tremble and can feel your body. A small black house behind you has grown hugely—and is lifting— it now stands firmly some feet above the ground, suddenly blindingly white. If only the fear you first felt would return, for dread and terror has come in its place with wire spaghetti all over, rolled up like barbed wire?

Then, gratefully, you wake up—bathed in sweat. You don't want to experience this again. But wouldn't you like to remember a fraction of it?

Such dreams are filled with ideas which can be the raw material from which creative works are fashioned. Their very unlikeliness takes you out of the ordinary—you have the stuff from which to make creative products. And even frightening dreams can be creative. Just recall the dream of Elias Howe and his successful sewing machine which wouldn't sew: until that frightening dream of being in the midst of savages ready to cook him—with their penises sticking out. He needed to convert the dream of the hole at the end of the penis into a hole at the end of a needle so that his successful sewing machine could really sew.

But how do you remember your dreams?

We have all had the experience of having had what we thought were significant dreams at the time we dreamed them. Often we thought they were vital, prophetic; warning us to protect something or to do something and thus ward off an evil event. Or, we would like to savor again a specially thrilling or erotic dream.

But shortly after we awake, most dreams are forgotten. Even your analyst would be pleased if you could recall your dreams and share them. The analyst might then learn something helpful about you.

We do have ways of helping us remember our dreams. And the more often we remember them the more successful we will be with each succeeding time.

(1) First, have a pad of large-sized sheets of paper and a pen next to your bed where you can reach out, even without looking, and grasp them.

(2) Then, in the stage when you have just about awakened from a dream and before opening your eyes, repeat the dream verbally to yourself loud enough so that you can hear it. This fixes it in your mind because you are getting an input via an additional route, i.e., aurally, by hearing it.

(3) Then, write it out. If you can write out at least the key words before you open your eyes you will be better able to trigger recollection of a greater number of elements of the dream. By opening your eyes, you get a disturbing visual input—furniture, familiar objects—which has nothing to do with your dream and tends to erase it. In fact, by opening your eyes, you largely cancel the advantages you have gained by reciting the dream verbally. Talking refers to the dream; seeing your familiar surroundings has nothing to do with your dream. Dreams are diaphanous curtains that can easily be torn.

(4) If you wake up at night to record a dream, *do not put on the light*—it banishes dreams. Write in the dark and feel your way. You will become accustomed to it.

(5) After you have followed this method every night— and we dream in spurts throughout the night—it will become increasingly easier to remember much of your dreams and record them. And only after you have had considerable experience in recording your dreams you can make it even easier: You may be able to use a ballpoint pen that has built into its writing end a weak light. It will

illuminate, mildly, the space on which you are writing. It will be helpful if you have already developed the propensity of writing with your eyes closed or half-open yet not losing the substance of the dream.

The reason for a pad of *large-sized* sheets of paper is obvious now: You can write larger so that your notes do not run together, which can make them illegible even to you. That becomes especially likely if you write words in the same space on which you have written before. Remember: Your eyes are still closed while you're writing.

Thus memory and recall are tools to help our creativity. If you expect to remember and practice remembering, you will gain experience in remembering, but more important, you will get to believe in your memory. Nothing is lost either in nature or in memory. It is only a question of relaxing and retrieving your memories. And remember this: It gets easier to remember the more you practice doing it.

(*See* Chapter 13, "Right Brain-Left Brain in Creativity.")

Science and Insight

True science teaches, above all, to doubt and
be ignorant.

Miguel de Unamuno (1864–1936)
—*The Tragic Sense of Life.*

Almost automatically the word *science* calls forth a reaction of awe from the average or even not-so-average person who is not a scientist. Next, we leap to the belief that when something is *scientific* it is valid for that reason alone. Just notice the variety of advertisements offering *scientific* rug cleaning, *scientific* rodent extermination, *scientific* removal of excess hair. These ride on the sacred cow aspect that science conveys to the layman.

It is true that these developments have been devised by science—or perhaps more properly, technology. It would be absurd for us to banish science like a political party that has lost an election. But the awe with which science is looked upon rubs off on the words of scientists, even the nonsense they may spout is considered scientific.

We cannot, and should not, condemn the role of science as such. It would be making the same mistake as that of endowing science with miraculous qualities. Science, as such, is said to search for truth, while it simply searches for facts. Now at the time of a discovery or development, a newly found so-called "fact" may be true—or at least believed to be true. But often it is an evanescent truth, which

is not truth at all because it is supplanted by another truth
when a subsequent discovery pushes the vaunted truth into
desuetude. For example, many scientific *truths* in medicine,
chemistry, etc. are examples of this. What was in the text-
books thirty or forty years ago is largely untrue now,
newer truths have supplanted them. No student could pass
an examination today in most scientific subjects were he to
study the good books of a generation ago.

Thus, seeking the truth sounds better than seeking facts.
There is doubt if the *facts* actually remain facts in the next
generation.

But science has contributed greatly to mankind. No one
would deny that. We can wage war more effectively thanks
to science. Having conquered certain diseases we have increased life expectancy. The "fact" that we have increased
longevity and at the same time decreased employability is
due to our veneration of another idol—the youth culture—
and is not the fault of science. We should pass the buck to
sociology or elsewhere; some logical scapecoat can be developed with a little assiduous application.

But then there are those who decry science completely. If
you go to either extreme, you will have very little trouble
in developing fanatical pronouncements, for things are
usually not just black or white. There may well be spiritual
bankrupcy in our utter materialism, but while we are spirit-
ually hungry, we must also nonetheless remain alert for our
own survival. We cannot deny the usefulness of science nor
banish it even if for the simple reason of keeping up an
international political pace and possible peace. Countries in
the Soviet orbit are using science to the utmost to surpass
us economically and politically.

But there is more to science than science. Science thrives
on ideas, springs from them. To refine those ideas we use a
method of procedure called *science*. And science in testing
a new hypothesis uses a party line—the scientific method, a
four-step procedure composed of observation, classification
of facts, formulation of hypotheses, and verification by experiment. It rose in the seventeenth century to avoid reli-
ance on authority ("Aristotle says so") or tradition ("It
was always done that way"). No idea can be taken seri-

ously unless it is amenable to an experimental test. The suppression of new ideas, even wild ones, under the banner of science is inquisitorial.

While often useful to separate the chaff from the wheat by insisting upon the ability to duplicate a result, when the scientific method as a rigid discipline enters into the very genesis of ideas—creativity—it is suppressing.

For example, even Alfred North Whitehead (1867–1947), the English mathematician and philosopher, saw that the role of the mathematics, straight science, had its limitations when he said: "There can be no true physical science which looks first to mathematics for the provision of a conceptual model. Such a procedure is to repeat the errors of the logicians of the Middle Ages."

The obvious conclusion is that science—or expertise—however "scientific" can be inimical to creativity. André Bennett, comparing science and creativity, epitomizes it well when he states that "Innovation, by its very nature is compatible [with science] while creativity is antithetical to commonly held beliefs."

This is a reasonable deduction, for creativity is nurtured upon intuition and insight. Science is circumscribed by rules, and there are no known rules for insight, according to Joseph Turner, an editor of *Science*.

Science can be used to refine what is known, but it cannot be used with any degree of effectiveness to study what is unknown. In fact, if the scientific method were to be rigidly followed there would be no progress, as the scientific method tests each previous step.. And if there is no step yet on the staircase of knowledge it does not bend itself well to study by the scientific method. In other words, Turner is saying that creativity is largely based on hunches, and controlled experiments kill hunches.

Science is not a replacement for imagination and cannot replace it any more than imagination is a replacement for scientific rigidity. Thus, it is clear that science based upon an extrapolation from present ideas is antithetical to creativity. In other words, science basing itself on "facts" cuts itself off from one of the extraordinary attributes of the mind, namely intuition, and the average scientist is un-flinchingly and inexorably wedded to facts.

Seeing the accustomed in an unaccustomed setting was customary with Albert Einstein—very definitely an above-average scientist. He invented or imagined situations and placed them over an observation he had already made. He said he had come upon the vision of his relativity theory by remembering how as a child when he was riding a train, everything he saw outside the window appeared to be moving backward as the train moved forward gathering speed. With the magic lantern of insight, Einstein saw and discovered a new vision, an explanation that was contrary to what the then-existing dogma held to be immutable.

Science does not thrive on gadgets but grows on ideas, namely insight and intuition, which are the genesis of ideas. Knowledge does not spark the creative mind without that explosive material that bursts into a creative idea.

What is the material that provides the creative fire-works? A removal away from the accustomed rut for one thing, thus providing yourself with a different vision and a new vantage point. To illustrate this, think of seeing things in a simple childlike way. This will open a magic lantern on a heretofore dark corner of views and ideas. You will look at things that as an average adult you wouldn't see.

One of the best ways we can nurture creativity is *simply not to suppress it*—let go, let it fly free. And don't worry about what the superannuated Mrs. Grundys of the Establishment will say: They will not like it. For the average mind never takes kindly to an idea that may cast doubt on the cherished established dogmas. Have courage and the return from your creative leap will pay you boundlessly in self-esteem and self-confidence as a person.

CHAPTER 26

Summary: You're on the Way

Several times I have been asked what one piece of advice I would choose with which to wish a reader godspeed and send him on his way toward enhancing himself through creativity. Forced to choose one I would say, *Don't be afraid of failing.* Failing, at first, can be a learning experience. To put it better, you should *Fail to fear, but don't fear to fail.*

But were I not limited I would add:

THINGS NOT TO DO.

(1) Remember the man sitting in an armchair gritting his teeth and clenching his fists—the picture of anxiety? When asked what he was doing, he answered through his teeth, "I am trying hard to relax." The point: Don't try so hard. Let it happen. Just hang loose mentally and physically and it will come.

(2) The secret is don't censor your thoughts. Let them roam freely. Woolgather, daydream. No thought is ridiculous, it may be productive. Don't censor yourself nor be ashamed of what first comes to mind.

(3) Don't be ashamed of what so-and-so will say. Don't fear ridicule. There are always people ready to tear down someone who has the courage they lack to venture into uncommon areas—and especially the courage to continue. If your spouse laughs at you, and that can be painful, stick out your tongue at him/her. Family dynamics are frequently so competitive that one spouse, in a bid for power

196

or domination, does not want to see his/her spouse succeeding. It is upsetting to the one who seeks domination and it loosens the planks on the power platform. What do you do? Laugh back—stick out your tongue. Don't be shamed or allow yourself to be pulled down. Don't try to use logic or reason with a spouse that tries to hold you down, you cannot reason with such emotions.

(4) And don't argue against yourself. Don't tell yourself that someone must have thought of, or even done before, the very thing you are trying to do. Even if someone did, the creative attitude on your part will result in an enhancement of you, your self-esteem, your self-actualization, your growth.

(5) You will find that when you learn a new rhetoric, those words expressive of events in creativity, you will have a new, enriched language with which to express your new sensations. And as you develop your ability to verbalize you will slowly be able to bring ideas forth. To paraphrase Nietzsche, "To name a thing is to bring it forth."

(6) Thus, you will enter a nonlogical dimension of prescience. Your *perceptual set* will be broadened. You will evoke, elicit, hence you will be able to describe feelings of spontaneous illumination. Through your newly found spontaneity you will find it easier to do instinctual improvisation. In that way you will enrich your sensory apparatus and the sensuous will be in sharper focus—as if you cleaned the windows of vision on your emotions. Then, after raising a sensation from the subliminal to the conscious or doing level, you may be able to step back and see the items of your own creativity.

THINGS TO DO

(1) Surrender to the voice inside of you—your intuition. Listen to your inner self. (Assuming you are not psychotic.)

(2) Ignore what the critics say.

(3) *DO* be active not passive; "doing something" helps banish fears, uncertainties, anxieties.

(4) Relax, be receptive to the inner world by relaxation. See things in your mind's eye. Use any form of relaxation,

such as TM, RR, or others outlined in this book. If you wish, try other methods not outlined in this book, such as hypnosis, it may just strike a chord in you.

Talk to yourself, verbalizing what troubles you and considering the alternatives. Talk to yourself in a mirror if it allows you to relax and relate to yourself. You may become possessed by an idea, and that is one component of creativity.

Picture for yourself in your mind's eye what it is that you want to accomplish, gain, produce, create. And don't worry if you start with a mess, for chaos has an order in itself; you will then rearrange the order.

(5) One of the things we have been taught is that if we work hard enough we will succeed. In some areas, yes, provided that you have the contact as well as the competence. Remember the picture of the man at the beginning of this chapter who is trying hard to relax? In the area of creativity *by doing less you do more.*

Appendix

This part, the Appendix, consists of several of my articles that have previously appeared in periodicals. They deal with creativity or other facets of the subjects discussed in this book. At times, I have made reference to them in Part 1 or Part 2 of this book.

These articles have been included and placed in this appendix because I believe they will serve as illustrative material, on a deeper level, for those interested.

Some of these articles are written in professional jargon, as much as I had wanted to avoid that. Nonetheless, they appeared in scientific publications and, as is the custom, convention calls for stuffiness—and the gutting of most humor.

But surely the reader interested in this subject on a deeper level will have the motivation to read on, and with just a little application should have no trouble understanding the *scientese*. Actually, *federalese* is worse.

Myth & Metaphor

Myth is a four-letter word in our orientation of scientific materialism. While *myth* merely denotes something legendary, an unfortunate connotation has grown up around it in giving it the aura of something spurious. In fact, the word *mythomania* means pathologic lying.

But there is a human need for myths; they are often symbols of a deeper and recondite truth. Man is also a symbol-making animal. Although we readily agree that he needs symbols and we accept their use in such endeavors, as say, mathematics or physics, we recoil from them in many other areas with the opprobrium that they are mystical.

Myths often express deep and hidden truths which become plain by viewing them as metaphors. Note, for example, many Biblical myths with their often-inherent wisdom pertaining to the human condition, as for example, *there is a time for every purpose, a time to be born, a time to die, a time to plant, a time to pluck* (Eccles. 3:1).

That the element of timing in human activities influences their success or failure is obvious. Another example is the action of casting bread upon the waters said to redound to the benefit of the donor. One should bear in mind that no cultures or religions have long endured without myths. Even Sparta—unemotional and pragmatic as it was—had myths in the constellation of its culture.

While man pursues the current vogue of the realm, *i.e.*, scientific materialism, he nevertheless finds that he needs other influences as those taught by myths with their often metaphorical meaning to gain meaning in his own life. Some find the beloved person. Others, fearing personal commitment, find something impersonal, as "humanity" to which they turn. But many have the intrinsic need to transcend themselves by devotion to something outside of the material sphere—as the occult for example, and *occult* has also been downgraded by connotations: it merely means something hidden, not necessarily something supernatural, infernal, or necromantic.

Myths form a strong support for ethics, decency, and much of the enduringly good that religion teaches. As soon as man demythologizes his beliefs they lose much of their influence, through being intellectualized. Note, for example, the theologic demythologizing of Jesus. In fact, abnegation of many myths throughout the centuries has had comparatively little constructive effect, because such abnegation or destruction of myths is soon followed by an emptiness on the part of man. Thus myths fill man's spiritual needs without which he becomes weary of the world and its accoutrements—or develops a sterility expressed in such philosophical constructs as reductionism. Even reductionists do not deny, though they decry, that man has emotive propensities. Myths speak to those emotive propensities—and allow man a figurative way to express the unknown, through his myth-making proclivity. In the emotive areas it does not really matter if myths are true—they give a man a way of expressing matters of the soul, emotions, feelings, elations, and sadness.

With the decline of myths, our old enchantments fail but our need for enchantment remains. It is in that way that myths give us the flavor of sublimity, of transcendence. They, too, are a reality but in a different sphere and in a different language or different coin.

When man set aside his myths to understand and create his world rationally, when, to use Max Weber's famous term, he "disenchanted" his world, the paradoxical result was, and is, irrational. Each piece of the modern world—each corporation, each post office, each army, each school, each little time-motion-studied part of every division of labor job—is a masterpiece of rational thought. But who would be so foolish to argue that these logically conceived pieces fit together in a rational whole? We live in a chaos of incontrovertible reasons, in a fog of discretely blinding clarities.

The word *rational* is a different language or coin, and one cannot understand the world of myths with a rationalistic approach; myths are not rational in that sense. Nor, in fact, is man in many of his actions rational.

And even Kant says that we cannot derive a universal significance from rational categories. While our man-made universe is a composite of rational categories, when one attempts to reconcile them, one finds chaos. For example, when one tries to reconcile what man *holds* to be good, with what he *does*, one derives a chaotic picture. This is well exemplified by Koestler's discussion of Paul Mac-Lean's hypothesis of our triune brain. For example, when man is God-oriented he is said to be irrational in the reductionist sense of the term. But without a God-orientation he is merely a metabolic machine—through a wondrously constructed one, as such, I am speaking of the ineffable concept of God, not of the constructs of the Church.

There is an analog to the myth: the metaphor. Literal-minded people are at a loss with metaphors. Derived from the Greek word *metapherein*, "to transcend" or "to transfer," our finite minds can encompass a metaphor and by its vehicle express certain feelings or concepts through it. Metaphors often serve as analogies or express a framework. Revelation comes in the clothes of a metaphor. For example, when we think of light we can express it in the sense of Genesis, or transcend it in the sense of photosynthesis.

We have further reified many metaphors to appeal to our understanding. For example, whether we speak of Mary Magdalen, Hero and Leander, Heloise and Abelard they are all reified metaphors for love.

Hegel well exemplified logic by defining it as "the money of the mind"—the coin by which the mind makes its transactions. That does not mean that logic is the *stuff* of the mind any more than money is the stuff of exchange—it is only the medium, or symbol, and we must guard against confusing the symbol with its object. To use the above metaphor, myth is the money of the emotions, or of the soul.

It is in this fashion that metaphors and myths enrich man's lives, reduce his *horror vacuii*, and enable him to transcend in a small measure the benality of his affluent though impoverished daily existence.

What Are We Living For?

This is the title of a book. Far beyond that it is a transcending question that we fear to ask ourselves, and when we do immediately close the question like a dirty book in which we may be immersed when a proper maiden aunt unexpectedly comes upon us. It may not be a comfortable question because we do not have a unitary answer. Often we cancel it from our minds—except that on reflection it recurs, silently, wordlessly, inevitably.

People often feel that it is a self-destructive question and that its macabre note is perhaps better fit to the ideations of Baudelaire, than to a "normal" sensible person. That would be fine—but it just is not so.

People ask themselves the question in many forms. And commensurately, they often act out various answers. For example, St. Augustine doubtless asked himself the question from the depths of his profligacy—and found something worthwhile to live for as another persona, i.e., as the Bishop of Hippo. In our own time, Yokio Mishima, probably the most accomplished Japanese writer and a Nobel Prize nominee, answered the question for himself by ritual, histrionic suicide. Possibly he asked the question, but, unable to separate himself from a profound self-centeredness, he did not draw even a tentative answer.

Also in our own time and within the last three generations, sound businessmen, after achieving outstanding successes, had reassessed themselves and their striving and drew answers that moved them to reduce active acquisition and turn their assets to good works. In religion it is called redemption; in theology, syncretism; in psychiatry often expiation—depending on what mirror you use. In cynicism it is called do-goodism or the three ages of man: get on, get honest, get honor—more evidence of the moral bankruptcy of cynicism.

There are no rigid answers—but the search must go on for our well being.

I said at the outset that the question, "What are we living for?" is the title of a book.* The author, Dr. Chauncey Leake, pharmacologist extraordinary, is in fact a Renaissance man, which is clear from his expertise in the numerous areas in which he is active. However, we are not testing the man but his book, and I would like to recount, or rather summarize, his insightful handling of the nuclear question, *What are we living for?* Even if you do not find new *facts* in the book regarding philosophy and its history, despite that, or perhaps because of it, if your experience parallels mine you will derive precious insights. And who can tell how insight becomes transmuted into inspiration? I should also mention that the instant book is part of a trilogy: the present book is on the ethics and the remaining two will be devoted to the logics and the esthetics.

To start answering the question, *What are we living for?*, Leake says to please the Big Boss. The Big Boss may be the mother attending her infant, then a parent, teacher, employer, God—he typifies the Big Boss as those to whom we feel beholden or whom we fear to offend. When you think back you will recall the elaborate superstructure and rituals we develop at different times of our lives to please the Big Boss—one of the reasons we may be living for.

From this simple notion you can readily see how we develop concepts of sin, responsibility, loyalty, group welfare, personal sacrifice—and even become true believers. And, indeed, Leake leads us through these concepts, their histor-

* *What Are We Living For: Practical Philosophy. 1. The Ethics* by Chauncey D. Leake, Ph.D., Sc.D., L.H.D., LL.D. 1973. $7.95. 185 pages. P.J.D. Publications, Ltd, 10 Oakdale Drive, Westbury, N.Y. 11590.

ical developments, and their mutations which we recognize in our contemporary world.

Conflicts will arise in fundamental questions such as these especially when we want to reserve individual goodies for ourselves and get individual pleasure which at times may not be consistent with the corporate or common good. This is hedonism which has been a form of conduct in various civilizations but first codified by Epicurus and in fact, *epicurean* has become a form of speech. Hedonism, contrary to popular belief, is not just lawless abandon but merely a let-me-do-my-own-thing-because-I-like-it approach to ethics. Note the relationship to the contemporary scene.

The various ethics offer a guidance from which we as people choose what pleases us or perhaps what is least in conflict with ourselves. But there usually does remain the eternal conflict with what responsible men *want* to do (to please themselves) and what they *must* do to (to please the Big Boss). This may well be basic to the ambiguities which are the source of many of our troubles not only with others, but with ourselves.

Leake is an empathic guide in the various other ethics. Readers of his book may well ask *why can't philosophy always be like that?* The answer is that it can be and it is, until the pedants encrust it with verbal barnacles to intellectualize it and make it a recondite language. After all, pedants must be saying to themselves, you should not treat civilians like equal people. In his clear and unpretentious fashion, Leake leads the reader through the various ethics; for example, through Stoicism, common in the Greek world which, contrary to popular belief that its main thrust is keeping a stiff upper lip, actually espouses self-examination, knowledge, and humanity. It is well to remember that humanity was practiced in a limited and unique way in the Greco-Roman world, as for example in relation to slaves. Although bought and sold the same as in other parts of the ancient world they were treated as human beings and perhaps responded as people, and often added to the intellectual life around them. For example, Aesop was a slave.

In urging us through our trek through the ethics, Leake further conducts us briefly through compassion—exemplified by Jesus and Hillel, through what I choose to call the ethics of compulsion as exemplified by St. Paul who packaged a best seller: sin.

But the pendulum swung. The Renaissance set the stage for skepticism and humanism flavored by the ethics of power by Machiavelli, which, in turn, was almost expected (by hindsight) to veer to the Reformation and Calvinism with its Puritan ethic.

In the matter of professional ethics Leake has a bold approach: is it *ethic* he asks or is it *etiquette?*—vastly different questions—and is it based on pragmatism? Call it sin, or call it ethics, people use altisonant names to discourage others from inquiring into our own motives. Again, is it ethics or is it etiquette?

The book contains more. It also deals briefly with our new sex ethic, situational ethic which we so greedily accept in order to rationalize our behavior and to make us feel less ambivalent. Prophetically, he speaks of Watergate—not by that name, of course—but enters into the roles of spying, corruption, and the ubiquitous conflicts of interest. I should note, however, that his tone is not hortatory but descriptive, sometime Socratic, always stimulating. Every man has conflicts of interest throughout his life—even in attempting to create an amicable aura between his wife and his mother. How we handle conflicts is the rub.

Does Leake answer the question *What are we living for?* To find his own approach I urge you to read his book. But, finally, every man must answer the question for himself, for after he satisfies his main drives for food and the self-preservation of his species including his sex drive, he does ask himself, *after that, what?* I hope that everyone finds his own affirmative and joyous answer but that no one is moved to say that what he is living for is because he is afraid to die.

What Does One Do for Fun?

A reasonably reliable way to assess the tone and tenor of the people of a previous era or past civilization is to try to find out what they did for fun. One can discover this from artifccts or other means; but you cannot invariably get definitive answers. When you find a strange ancient musical instrument it does not necessarily mean that music or its variants was the fun thing. For example, primitive razors were found in the ruins of Pompeii which were buried in the lava of Vesuvius in about 80 B.C., but this does not mean that people shaved for fun.

Translated into an individual level we commonly think that the most fun had by ancient or modern people is through sexual activity. As a matter of fact, by and large, sex is the third most common activity among people. It is preceded, according to some cultural anthropologists, first by dancing, and second by drug taking. When we consider that dancing is commonly part of a religious ritual, especially in the populous Far East, it is not hard to imagine. Similarly, drug taking is also commonly part of a religious ritual; we need only to think of khat, or the drugs taken by African tribes as part of their rituals, to accept that attractive notion. Actually, to drug taking we must add alcohol—a drug that has little to recommend it except that, in common with other drugs, it is taken to produce euphoria or oblivion or both.

But is that all? After that, what?

Man continues to search for a state which we variously

call happiness, satori or other forms of illumination, even nirvana, though he does not even hope to reach it. In this attempt he enters gingerly and chaotically into the preternatural.

There are those who attempt to reach this state through other means, for example by striving to multiply the good things they already have. People may have a marvelous practice or business, both a happy marriage and an undemanding mistress, children who though teenagers do not act as if papa is antiquated or otherwise superannuated, a princely house, and a boat that sleeps 10. To enhance their fortune they live up to it with other thrills such as sartorial splendor or a safari—not merely pedestrian travel—or a ski trip which ends right in front of their own lodge in Colorado which they built for the purpose.

But after that, what?

Still the search for happiness, fulfillment, or whatever you call it goes on, apparently because the bill is not filled though the cup runneth over, in the search for euphoria and, barring that, oblivion. Manhood is as much equated with the money a man makes as by his sexual potency.

Perhaps we are asking the wrong questions or looking into wrong directions to find that indefinable we-know-not-what. Man, by and large, feels more fulfilled when he is able to accomplish something in an area beyond his usual day-to-day activity, or even in his daily endeavor when he brings into it a certain explosive ferment that beatifies existence. I submit that the ferment may be, and the answer may possibly lie in creativeness.

There are various types, expressions, or manifestations of creativeness. The word calls to mind an artistic creation whether it is a painting, a book, or doing something with your hands which is in vogue, or *in*, like sculpture. It also calls to mind creative carpentry or creative gardening or other activities which have the word *creative* stuck in front of them. My own view is—and many will dispute it—that often these creative activities are merely forms of occupational therapy.

To many, creativeness is most satisfying if they can bring it into the compass of their everyday lives in their work, which then becomes a fun thing as well as a rewarding occupation. This can be done through the medium of a certain kind of thinking, namely, seeing an ordinary problem in an extraordinary way and solving it ingeniously. It does not matter how unimportant the application may be; it becomes a truly creative act when man has been able to transcend with outstanding effect that which he has been taught. Basically, *it is not the thing but the thought* that rewards.

For example, a way of problem solving that is truly a creative endeavor is *lateral thinking*. It is not our accustomed logical, syllogistic approach to a problem but one in which the mind divests itself of the so-called common sense remedies.

Here is an illustration of lateral thinking. A new office building has been completed and tenants filled it in a short time. Only then was it found that a certain bank of elevators was insufficient to carry the traffic that developed. The common sense thing to do is to build more elevators. Fine, but there were no extra shafts. Another would be to put into service additional elevators which served other floors. But that would create the same problem in the bank of elevators from which one was pressed into service to relieve the congestion in the first bank. Another logical thing would be to clear out some tenants to relieve the congestion. Indeed, that would work but part of the rental would be lost. The problem still remained: how do you enable people to wait for one of the two elevators without climbing the walls?

A think tank type of problem solver suggested covering the marble walls next to the elevators with large mirrors. Idiotic, wasn't it? Of course it worked. People seeing their full image in the mirrors became preoccupied with their appearance and forgot the long wait.

I have come across a book on lateral thinking which is one of the most productive ones I have read in years. It is called *Po: A Device for Successful Thinking*, by Edward De Bono (218, pp. $5.95, Simon & Schuster, 630 Fifth Ave., New York, N.Y. 10020, 1972).

The word *Po* does not mean anything—it is merely a

symbol. But Po has to do with thinking and problem solving through lateral thinking in your work, in fact, in your life. This is a creative endeavor which the individual himself devises—not the occupational therapy sort of busy work to use idle time.

In a few words: historically and traditionally we think in an order of fixed logic, aided by our previous experiences. (Experience can become at times the worst equipment to put into problem solving. How do you know that the particular experience upon which you rely is parallel to the current problem? It may so appear to be clearly on the surface, but to the intrinsic makeup of the current problem it may bear no versimilitude.)

De Bono, the author, calls the conventional fixed logic the Yes/No game and decries it. He even negates dialectical reasoning which often has been successful from Hegel on. Instead, he says, in the preoccupation with our processes of thinking we pay little attention as to *how we first perceive a problem*. We must first perceive something before we can think about it. He also denigrates the current mania about relevance. It is plain that the so-called relevance, even by definition, precludes a new ingenious solution because it deals with the accustomed or orthodox way of viewing things.

According to De Bono, here is a comparison between the Yes/No and the Po systems: *No* is the basic tool of the logic system; *Yes* is the basic tool of the belief system; *Po* is the basic tool of the creative system. (He speaks of *Po* as if it were the *only* approach to creativeness—with which I differ for a number of reasons—but it has enduring advantages.)

Many examples are given. One simple example from the book as to how we perceive things: when a car overheats we immediately think of adding water to the radiator. But we do not easily perceive the holistic picture: it may not be lack of water but lack of circulation in the cooling system due to a slipping fan belt. There are many other examples. (The previous account of putting mirrors on walls to *hasten* elevators is not from the book.) But many other caveats to our thinking are given in the book, such as, the sequence trap, where a frozen pattern in our thinking precludes a solution because the feedback deforms the problem itself.

But I must confess considerable annoyance with the slow pace of the book and the author's overselling his system. He doesn't need to do that—it speaks overwhelmingly well for itself. But that is a small penalty to pay for the stuff it offers in the unchartered forest of creativeness.

Will this book fulfill you, give you happiness, fill the gnawing disaffections you may have? Probably not. Solutions come from within. But the material it contains may well enable you to find a type of creativeness by offering a way of apprehending things—or a personal creativeness.

Poetry and Creativeness

Poetry is, first, an emotional experience. By convention it is also a literary form. Its practitioners fall into poetry as into one of the rites of passage common to the puberty rites among aborigines. While the poet does not whirl like a dervish in his practice of poetry, he nonetheless seeks a divine afflatus, an exaltation, or a revelation. Some wish to stimulate the divine afflatus or to sustain its presence longer. Others seek to make it appear in soil hitherto sterile. Through the use of alcohol, absinthe, opium, and other drugs—and, more recently, psychotropic agents—some have escaped into a psychotic state in order to receive the poetic stimulus. Others have attempted to enter into "other consciousness," to use the words of William James, or into "other categories," to use Ouspensky's.

Much attention has been given to the person of the poet in the attempt better to understand what fulmination occurs in him preceding the creation of a poem, or what precipitates the emotional experience a poem may represent. The study of the lives of the poets goes off at times, however, on a biographical or biological tangent rather than on an exploration of the realm of poetry. Keats may have expressed the difficulty: "A poet is the most unpoetical of anything in existence because he has no identity—he is continually in, for, and filling some other body—sun, moon, sea."

And poetry has been ill-served by many—even by its own devotees. For example, rhyme is one of poetry's greatest assets, but rhyme has also done poetry a disservice by creating two anomalous streams. One, poetry-rhyme has by inversion became rhyme-poetry, where even execrable verse is called poetry as long as it rhymes; and, two, reaction against enslavement to rhyme has produced literary abortions that emerge limbless and lawless, without beauty or purpose except, perhaps, to shout out their liberation from traditional forms. This reaction is not a matter of an abomination of form alone; many of those reformers have nothing to say in the first place. While we espouse the belief that poetry is an emotional experience before it is a literary form, we do not believe that contortions for the sake of an avant-garde form create poetry. It is difficult to give the impression of incandescence when there is no light. The question of rhyme-poetry is in fact an old one. Thomas Campion (1567–1620) attacked rhyme as a hallmark of poetry. Apparently this became a cause célèbre, for Samuel Daniel (1562–1619) wrote his "Defence of Ryme" as an apologia for rhyme.

That poetry is basically substance rather than a prescribed form is demonstrated in that God-haunted book, the Bible, which has no rhyme or prescribed lines but whose poetic nature is evident even to those who do not regard it as God-inspired.

While poetry is born of or can call forth strong emotional reactions, it must nevertheless be carefully and lovingly refined so that the final product will reflect its poetic quality. What poetry is *not:* an oracular expression that cannot be altered once it has been verbalized. It is not commonly an intellectual exercise, but it can be likened to music through its cadence or rhythm.

Beauty of language and lofty thoughts are, by and large, subjective notions; hence, what may appear to be beautiful and lofty to one may not appear so to others. People seek various qualities in poetry. For some it must have sheer, simple, unalloyed beauty in expression; for others it must carry a message; for still others it must be laden with emotion. Also, there are those who demand form irrespective of substance and others who seek substance and are only mildly concerned with form. Each of these may be right, in part, in what is regarded as poetry. But whether purpose, image, or message is considered the hallmark of poetry, poetry must have, above all, a *rhythm*, a *cadence*. This rhythm, or cadence, has a powerful influence on the emotions which poetry elicits. A musical analogy here is the march, to the strong rhythm of which the hearer reacts with strong martial emotion. In fact, some poets first experience a cadence which precipitates the creative encounter with a poem.

That poetry is an emotional experience suggests that more than one emotion can be called forth by a poem. This is true. A poem can illumine, inspire, infuriate; can transcend with a mystical aura; can suffuse the reader with a warmth beyond mere pleasure—depending, of course, on the creativeness or receptivity of the reader and his ability to react and to feel.

Writing a poem often serves the poet's psychological need; it can serve as a catharsis—or have an ameliorative effect. The reader, if receptive, also reacts emotionally, although perhaps not in the same degree as the poet. Perhaps because warmth and emotional lability constitute the basis of poetry we have the touching religious poetry of Juan de la Cruz, Francis Thompson, or Gerard Manley Hopkins; perhaps the outpouring of poetic material at revival meetings or in Negro spirituals or the folk songs of Leadbelly arises from easily shelved inhibitions. The wild exaltation and its expression, which comes from the feeling of nearness to the deity, is not parallel to the restraint in the "frozen" churches, although the formal churches from time to time crack the artificial restraints of civilization and break out in glossolalia. But in general there is considerably more nearness to the deity in the storefront Pentecostal churches than in the proper cathedrals, where the shouting of the ineffable name is frowned upon lest it lead to an unrestrained reaction. Perhaps the alienation of man from man arises from a suppression of such *affects*. And the same custom of restraint may have reduced today's interest in poetry, for poetry makes insatiable demands upon the inmost of man's emotions.

Poetry may thus serve as a powerful remedy against the

alienation between man and man and against the anomie of society. Poetry therapy may therefore not only minister to individual illness; it may also take its place as a therapeutic measure for a sick society—against the alienation between man and man and against the anomie of society.

Some rather bizarre happenings are reported in poems. The unusual fixes our attention and creates a sensation in us because it travels on tracks not commonly used in our daily lives—and rarely even in our idealized lives. Analyzing the transfixing power of a phrase in poetry is not productive, since we have not yet, except in general speculations, succeeded in assessing it. For example, the imagery in *Kubla Khan* is not unfamiliar in kind; yet the sensations Coleridge most likely felt and which the reader absorbs are beyond the effect of a simple anecdote. It is more than a visit of a man from Porlock. Similarly, the sketches of Aubrey Beardsley have a quality difficult to describe, and our attempt to verbalize it always leaves us dissatisfied. It is as if, after trying to draw a deep breath, we feel we have not plumbed the depths of our breathing capacity.

Similarly, trying to discuss the poetry of William Blake gives us a strong sense of the inadequacy of words. Perhaps the reason is that we use words on a superficial level and have no faith that they can match the depth of our feelings, which is *exactly* what poetry attempts to do, that is, to express in words the depth of our emotions. In that sense, too, poetry is an emotional experience.

And what about the creator of poetry—the poet? The stereotype of the poet is as common as that of poetry, although the stereotype changes with the times. Many great poets of the past are reputed to have been mad, for who but madmen could have had some of the visions inherent in poetry? Many poets—Blake and Baudelaire, for instance—are conceded to have been mentally or emotionally disturbed. But there were others who, although deeply sensitive, were presumably not emotionally disturbed. All great poets are alike in one respect: they are creative in almost any sense of the word. Perhaps in one sense all are inspired. Some of us see hallucinations implicit in poetry, but we may be merely smug in calling hallucinations those sublime visions conjured out of the imagination.

CREATIVENESS

If we are to term all poets "creative," we should be able to define the term by calling out those aspects associated with creativeness, for we best know creativeness *post hoc ergo propter hoc* (only by its result).

When the preconscious is sensitized, or highly perceptive, it reacts unpredictably and perhaps explosively in a way different from the so-called norm. That, perhaps, is the reason it is believed that seeing or sensing the old in a new way is a creative act. It follows, therefore, that the richer the storehouse of information and sensation, the more there is from which to draw.

Enriching that storehouse of information and sensations is possible by deliberate and systematic accumulation; but it is also likely that the information accumulated in this way will be wooden and will not lend itself to utilization. It may be an immobile reservoir. Perhaps there is a method in accumulation as there is a *way* of thinking or of *arranging* the acquired information. When one begins a systematic and deliberate acquisition of information simply for erudition's sake, that acquisition may be overselective, biased toward the pragmatic—and sterile.

The acquisition of seemingly *useless* information becomes at times one of the richest of gains. Creativeness is not a mechanical screening of ideas but is principally the manner in which a curious mind transforms the wealth of material it has beachcombed, retrieved, and transcended into art.

The *variety* of information in the mental storehouse enriches the ability of seeing the old in a new way. A rich leaven of so-called useless information may create the very ferment that triggers a creative act. The brain tends to record everything. But the creative faculty makes the selection of what it draws, or transforms and utilizes.

Retention of the fund of information requires memory for its storage—and the ability to recall, decode, and convert from a subconscious code into conscious verbalization.

This is the mobility of information and sensations previously mentioned. Retention—or memory—does not presuppose that the accumulated fund of information is thrown together helter-skelter like beans in a bag. Mobility is a factor. But order is the first law of the universe. There is usually an arrangement—with some indefinable guiding principle—probably differing from person to person. The arrangement is not rigid or frozen into cells like an ice-cube tray; it has, rather, a kind of elastic classification. There is order in thinking, but this order need not be rigid. It is an order which, while perhaps classified by subject and stored vertically, has a strong horizontal flow of intercommunication. An insulated, rigid, vertically stacked arrangement is not a mobile one, but vertical storage with free horizontal interchange *allows conveyance of information from one image or one set into another.*

Creativeness is said to rest upon insight. A passion or a compulsion possesses the poet—upon the revelation that insight represents. Jung well expressed this phenomenon: "Art is a kind of innate drive that seizes a human being and makes him its instrument."

The creative person in his act of creation is probably in a hypnoidal state. If this state is interrupted, the creative moment can flee. Note the classic example of the man from Porlock who knocked on Coleridge's door—thus breaking his sequence when he was writing *Kubla Khan.* This suggests clearly that creativity requires discipline, not abandon. Despite the face of spontaneity that a creative act may present, the spontaneity is based upon a subconscious or preconscious preparation. Coleridge's preoccupation before he sat down to write *Kubla Khan* bears this out.

Various poets express the idea of the process differently, but there is a general meeting of views. For example, Wordsworth's *spontaneous overflow of powerful feelings* and Spender's *concentration as a prelude to inspiration* appear to coincide in principle. Reason and logic—and the strange languages therein—are the veils which cover creativity; insight tears away the veils that cover or, worse, distort.

Biological scientists have attempted to evaluate creativity

or imagination in concrete terms according to the canons of the scientific method. Gerard, a neurophysiologist, has thus far epitomized that type of endeavor in terms which are far from concrete: "Creative imagination is an action of the mind that produces a new idea or insight." That is not essentially different from A. E. Housman's "Meaning is of the intellect—poetry is not."

MADNESS

Some splendid poetry has been written by the deranged. But it is not at all clear whether the poet was able to write poetry of superb caliber before he was deranged or whether it was only during the derangement that he was able to produce poetry of a lofty nature. As far as I am aware, no study of this question has been made.

Perhaps it may be well to oversimplify this complex subject by stating that the realm of fantasy does not belong solely to schizophrenics. The sensitive mind often takes excursions there to express itself—in poetry as well as in other arts. While schizophrenia has many faces, the biggest difference between the schizophrenic and the normal person is, perhaps, that the schizophrenic believes his fantasy and the latter realizes that his excursion is fantasy and returns to reality. (This is similar to the quip that the neurotic builds castles, and the psychotic lives in them.) This point is hopelessly complex, because schizophrenics may have varying degrees of insight. An excellent example of poetry of high caliber done by a schizophrenic:

PANIC

And is there anyone at all?
And is
There anyone at all?
I am knocking at the oaken door . . .
And will it open
Never now no more?
I am calling, calling to you—
Don't you hear?
And is there anyone

Near?
And does this empty silence have to be?
And is there no-one there at all
To answer me?

I do not know the road—
I fear to fall.
And is there anyone
At all?

[FRIEDA FROMM-REICHMANN, "Loneliness," *Psychiatry,*
February 1959]

As mentioned above, there have been many mad poets
(but many hatters were also mad). This does not, however,
mean that madness makes poetry or poets. Nonetheless, although the nature of the relationship is not clear there may
well be a relationship between madness and creativity.
There are two diametrically opposed views on this topic.
One, which L. J. Hatterer espouses, holds that madness de-
stroys the creative artist, and the other considers madness
to be a component of creativity, although it disclaims the
idea that creativity is a component of madness. The term
"madness" is here used as an omnibus term covering various degrees of neurosis, psychoneurosis, and even frank
psychosis. The cliché that madness and genius are allied is
commonplace. Aristotle and Dryden, among others, considered madness an occupational hazard of genius. Alexander
Cruden, mentally deranged nearly all his life, wrote the
monumental *Concordance of the Bible.* (In my view this is
not a creative work per se.) Benvenuto Cellini saw "efful-
gent light play on his personal shadow." Cowper described
his own lifelong melancholy—depression—in his Crazy
Kate, who "begs an idle pin of all she meets" (begging a
pin was a characteristic picture, in Cowper's time, of the
emotionally disturbed). Samuel Johnson in *Rasselas* described his own disturbances. Other indications of madness
can be discerned in the writings of Pope, Poe, Fielding,
Rousseau, Pascal—or in the delusions of Luther in his conversations with the Devil, or in the hallucinations of Des-

cartes despite his mathematical appraisal of the world. Shakespeare's characters are rich in descriptions of madness: Timon of Athens, Othello, Hamlet, Macbeth, King Lear, and others. Shakespeare was undoubtedly knowledgeable in the anomalies of emotional function, and there are those who ascribe his knowledge to personal derangement. Others violently oppose that imputation. Some, with Freud, contend that man's search is toward gratification and that art, because it is a substitute for gratification, is neurotic. Those who agree point out that, like amber, both are results of pathological processes.

LSD

That some drugs can produce exaltation and other states which resemble madness there is no disputing. The state brought on by these psychedelic (mind-manifesting) drugs is not, as is claimed, a replica of psychosis. Nonetheless, certain manifestations of madness and the effect of psychedelic drugs are similar or may even be identical.

For centuries man has attempted to stimulate his creative output through drugs. The transfiguration of the senses—in which, for example, sounds are seen and colors felt—is often an integral component of great poems. Since such alteration of sense perception takes place through LSD and other psychedelic drugs, the user may believe that these drugs are the transport medicine that will enable him to create great poetry.

People ordinarily take drugs in their desire for euphoria or oblivion. Since the advent of LSD, some persons have taken it in order to go on a "trip" which will disclose to them visions and experiences they have not known to exist because of the limits of their imaginations. Creative persons have also taken LSD and other psychedelic drugs to overcome a block in their creativity or to stimulate their creativity to greater heights. LSD, mescaline (peyote), hashish (cannibis, marijuana, pot), and opium are psychedelic drugs in descending order of effectiveness which have been or are used for enhancing creativity. Each of these drugs produces distortions in perception of space, time, or color; and hallucinations, delusional systems, or situation distor-

tions ranging from alienation of the familiar to warm iden-
tification with visions.

While we carefully refine, purify, and weigh the amounts
of psychedelic drugs administered, they interact with so
many other substances when taken into the body that they
defy specification. Therefore, except in very general terms,
it is not possible to state that a given psychedelic agent
creates a standard type of distortion or a duplicable set of
visions. These psychedelic drugs produce an altered state—
the type of alteration being greatly dependent upon the ego
structure or other affective states of the individual. In other
words, one cannot construct a chart of correspondence
which would list each drug and the specific images it produces—except broadly.

The emphasis of this article is on poetry and not on psychedelic agents. Nonetheless, it would be informative to relate the types of drugs taken by creative persons. Aldous
Huxley, whose devotion to mescaline is almost as well
known as his devotion to LSD, believes that "the schizophrenic person is like a man permanently under the influence of mescaline." The world of fantasy intrudes into the
real world, and the user cannot differentiate between them.
For example, among the changes in perception of reality in
schizophrenia is a distortion of the body image—there may
be a sensation of shrinking or of a huge growth with atten-
dant loss of boundary protection. Things simply seem unreal. There is often a feeling of depersonalization, and paranoid notions may produce rage as a reaction. There are
withdrawal from interpersonal contact, strange and unaccustomed and purposeless postures or movements of the
body, a sense of impending doom, the feeling of being controlled by an outside power, sudden and striking revelations which may be of a religious nature, and delusions regarding sight and hearing. To these incipient symptoms of
schizophrenia the sense distortion from mescaline is similar. For example, a change in body image may perhaps be
expressed poetically:

> I feel as if my person lifted
> Clear from my body-skin inside my house.

Or:

> Magnetic poles meeting
> Nullify the phases that draw:
> Whether they draw us across slime
> Or synthesis or starknaked drawings
> They draw the power of growth from our hair.
> Scenes of primeval magnificence,
> Lightnings that do not sear skin
> Precluding mountains that are passable
> Lying historians that are credible;
> Such visitations live our lives hundredfold
> Compensate our short hairs with hairy hides
> And multiply the numbers of our body.

It is reported by users of psychedelic drugs that commonplace objects take on new and exquisite meanings. The parallel to psychosis can be made. In the early development of the paranoid syndrome of schizophrenia a patient may find a commonplace mailing of a letter an act of epiphany—wherein he partly transmutes himself into the letter he mails, his voice resurrecting when the recipient reads it. Or, quite the opopsite, in an apocalyptic sense, he may see fire engines speeding down the street but will not associate them with a fire. He may perform his acts of daily living like a robot, their meaning or purpose lost; but on the other hand, he may be having mystical revelations. For example, a patient wrote:

> I found I all at once a pope became
> And knew that sluts and lust are not a sin.

Or:

> You appeared in black and white and in elux
> A color that is extraterrestrial
> Elux, the color not known on earth
> Like manna—a celestial fall—a terrestrial find.
> Framed in elux, the extraterrestrial color
> Stay! In your ray, all will allay, array.

The effects of LSD are similar to those of mescaline—but hugely accentuated. LSD is mescaline with a built-in arrowhead that enters deeply and disorganizes profoundly. The distortions with LSD are more widespread and the hallucinations more bizarre; common things take on a sacramental hue, and an apotheosis of normally insignificant objects often takes place. Yet, conversely, the most abject ego debasement may take place in the user's visions, and catastrophic panic may occur. A sense of invincibility may lead to self-destruction; for instance, a user may step into the path of a speeding car in the desire to stop it.

> The years add breath upon a heap of words
> Upon the structure of our responses
> Until each noiseless breath
> Evokes a signal like a bell.
> In concert, breaths sing out their symphony
> Or blare out their cacophony
> Some tinkle, clink, tick, jingle
> Others peal and roar, roll and boom.

With hashish there is an expansion of certain dimensions—time, space, affects. The emphasis is on colors. While there is distortion in substance, the principal distortions are in form. Literary users describe miraculous lands that arise—sybaritic visions full of luxury, peopled with servants and companions (usually not demons, although anxiety-producing hallucinations can occasionally occur). Manifestations appear to be more frequently those of grandeur than of squalor.

> A splendid image in splenetic gleams
> Broke from the habitat of coral beds,
> Freed from the crawling, slimy creatures
> That multiply themselves in pools of sponge,
> Freed from the counterpart of double life
> Epimetheus, into our midstream plunge.
> With your step you cover vast dominions
> Which when you step upon you blank them out. . . .

Or:

> Cyclop, satyr, entered for his potion,
> He dispensed them neverceasing slumber,

On me alone he forced a poisoned gall
And sank with skull and with rebounding fall
Through fourteen stages of his warming potion.
I rose, and feebly drank perennial numbers
I nodded twice, and joined the cyclop slumbers.
Or:

Mouldy earth and musty passion blender
Rebirth to you will come, 'fore horny cliffs
Will in the snow of frost seek a defender
From treacherous albatrosses. Or sluggish rivers
Floating from east again to east will spurt
Their waters, like the whales, to greenish clouds
To fire and purify themselves asunder.
Or in his callousness the lord of light will dart
An arrow from the east through my pallid nails
And stream the sun from all my fingertips
Do not scream when they have touched your lips.

The following list of poets matched with the drugs they
reputedly used does not show a predictable correspondence
between psychedelic agent and the nature of inspiration as
transmuted into poetry.

Charles Baudelaire	Opium, alcohol, hashish
Samuel Taylor Coleridge	Opium
Thomas De Quincey	Opium
Alexandre Dumas	Hashish
Théophile Gautier	Hashish
Allan Ginsberg	Hashish
Edgar Allan Poe	Alcohol
Arthur Rimbaud	Hashish, opium, absinthe
Paul Verlaine	Absinthe

The unfortunate myth has sprung up that psychedelic
agents, known to accentuate creativeness, will make a poet
of a sterile, emotionally flat, and shallow person. This is
untrue. Poetry may spring forth with proper stimulation *if*
there is an inner richness in which it spawns. It is perhaps
a transposition of what one is to what one sees and, hence,
expresses. A drug may stimulate, transport, or distort, but

it does not create or produce when the soul is hollow. Poetry may be hallucination, but it is also the reflection of a rich imagery, articulateness, and the ability to use the word forms to write it. It is not the ranting of a sterile man, hallucinating under the effect of a psychedelic drug. It is the weaving of exaltation, grandeur, ecstasy—even anxiety, anguish, agony—though fallow periods may inhibit its expression. Poetry resurges through insight—immanence becoming imminent—transcending into the verbal form called poetry.

Poets virtually transcend their finite selves when ready for the creative act. Schiller, it is reported, had an olfactory delusion (which arises in the limbic system), for he smelled rotten apples when he sat down to write. Regrettably, this does not mean that smelling rotten apples will lead to creativity. (Reprinted by permission of the University of Chicago from *Perspectives in Biology and Medicine* Vol 14; pp 639–650; Summer 1971.)

ADDITIONAL READING

T. DE QUINCEY. Confessions of an opium eater. Ed. E. Sackville-West. Chester Springs, Pa.: Dufour, 1950.

R. W. GERARD. Sci. Monthly, January 1946.

B. GHISELIN (ed.). The creative process. Berkeley: Univ. California Press, 1952.

E. M. GLASER. The physiological basis of habituation. New York: Oxford Univ. Press, 1966.

L. J. HATTERER. The artist in society: problems and treatment of the creative personality. New York: Grove, 1965.

A. E. HOUSMAN. The name and nature of poetry. New York: Macmillan, 1933.

C. G. JUNG. Modern man in search of a soul. New York: Harcourt, Brace, 1956.

J. L. LOWES. The road to Xanadu. New York: Random House, Vintage Books, 1959.

F. H. LUDLOW. The hasheesh eater. 1860.

S. SPENDER. Partisan Rev., Summer 1946.

Dream & Vision— Vision & Image—Reality

Many thoughts happen before we accept a notion. More often we find when a thought arises in our minds or hearts we either accept or abandon it. We can also let it lie fallow in indecision—in the storehouse where we send many of our ideas. In doing this we strengthen or weaken the nature or texture of each particular notion; and whether we convert it into a creative act depends on whether we want it to live in one of our three areas—thinking, doing or feeling.

But many such notions, I suspect, in some stage of their development become part of the deeper consciousness that is more fundamental than either of our intellectual or emotional spheres. This is perhaps a generic communal well, which is part of us all, from where we draw inspiration. This wellspring is our collective unconscious, our legacy as thinking, feeling, dreaming human beings. The language of dreams is the mother tongue of this underground of inspiration, and the words it uses to speak to us are the picture symbols of images and visions.

Thus, the dream is the basis of virtually all of our creativity—aspiration, action, accomplishments, and failures. But to wish to dream when we will it to happen is to court disappointment. Such is the surpassing fullness of life itself that the power to dream does not yield to wisdom, to propriety, to logic. The dream's spirit of life in the fact of certain death when we awake appears to give the dream an unspeakable luxuriousness as it forms despite the aura of its imminent end.

Those who are the killers of the dream—whether under the guise of wisdom or social propriety, duty, obligation to God and country, or guarding a crooked "realism"—are the killers of man. They match the dream with the fact: If the dream does not correspond with their definition of the fact, they kill the dream, as if the facts they see were the only sovereign thing in our world. A dream, in short, is *an intangible feeling in an intangible universe.* It does not yet have a setting, and is not circumscribed by a frame, nor frozen into a reference point.

Dream is, then, the indescribable vapor that pervades man's thinking. It frequently take a form, though that form is delicately hazy, and it is in its first stirring starting to become an entity. Transparent at first, it then becomes a vision. A vision *intangible in a tangible setting* has no form; it is merely a glimmer of an idea lighting up a dream, giving it tremendous power—a beginning. But it is the vision that lifts the dream from merely a preoccupation, into a possibility of existence. When a dream shakes the dreamer, seizes him, and he sees the world as if he had never really seen it before, he has been touched by a vision. At this moment the dreamer is urged to clear away the vapors that becloud the dream.

Touched by beyondness, the dream has been given a future, if you will, the vision becomes personalized into a visage. When we speak of the visage of the angel of mercy in the battlefield, this is an intangible picture set in a tangible setting. When we speak of the image of Christmas in the festive mood; this is a tangible picture placed in an intangible setting.

The visage and the image appear to us after the vapor of the dream has been dispelled by the vision. The visage and the image then begin to take a form and redeem the intangible imprisoned by the unreal, or rather that which has not yet become real but which may become real in the next step of development. A visage and/or image is the bridge between dream and reality. We must have an image as a frame of reference through which and against which we test the dream to see if it can stand as a source and parent of reality. Also we test to determine if the image can be converted into a reality.

At this point it is possible that a reverse action may take place, though logic or thinking cannot guide us. At this moment the visage and/or image can regress to a dream, and thus it will be destroyed and lost. If an image lacks the inner strength and quality to develop into reality this is a natural process of selection and rejection. But even a robust visage and image can be destroyed when we allow it by aimlessness to slip back or degenerate into a dream. Just as an image can regress to a dream, so reality can regress to an image. A return to a previous stage of development is involution and regression.

Reality—or the materialization of the image—is the consummation of the dream. It is a *tangible picture in a tangible setting*. It allows us to examine and evaluate the thing itself in the frame of reference it occupies. Such an appraisal redeems what has become the product itself from its inseparability from the processes that produced it.

Comparison is the assay we have by which we can assess, when standards or constants are unavailable to us. Those who do not compare the newly emerged reality with the image that produced it arrest further development. In fact, their reality may be merely a term; it may lack realness. Reality leans on the image, though it is independent of it and not related to it.

Somewhere during the transformation of the image into reality (with reality emerging more through reasoning and less through feeling) an obstacle course has to be run—a sort of trial by ordeal. Unfortunately, this does not test the goodness of the image or assess its worth for potential development into reality. On the contrary, it is the area where hostile elements operate, distort, and deform the image, twisting it into a caricature of reality.

One of those elements harmful to the orderly development of image into reality is inconsistency; another is change of meaning or change of aim; a third is rationalization. A fourth element may be argument brought forth for reasons of convenience or intellectual dishonesty, such as when assessing a statement one were to ask unreasonably, "Says who?" instead of, "Says what?" A fifth element may be the inability to resist reaching for the glitter of cleverness. One cannot live without thought for the next day and expect to develop the larger canvas of a life. Allegorically, the minute lacks dimension, proportion, and perspective. To settle for the immediate means one misses these qualities, all present in the larger scope of an overall endeavor, and make life and dreams enduring.

Reality is not necessarily the same as facts, for in the realm of the nonmaterial, facts are worthless coin. Reality may also be an abstract concept defined in concrete terms, as for example in the question, should men pattern their conduct on the legend of the gods or should they act as humans.

Our limitations in thinking, feeling, perceiving, and articulating—coupled with our intense desire to see "results" or answers—often rushes us into declaring as an answer merely an intermediate stage of the answer or a part of an answer. We can easily enough declare a stage, an event, or a thought *to be* reality and release ourselves from further search. That is all the more likely to happen if the stage, event, or thought of the moment appears for the moment to be agreeable or acceptable and in line with our ingrained prejudices and habits that we are unwilling to give up. By merely affixing a name, we do not make the name descriptive or even indicative of what we propose it represents.

Perhaps reality cannot be defined by inclusion. But we can partially define it by exclusion. It is not necessarily that which is at one with our aim. Our aim may lack reality.

Then, too, we frequently find merely a supplement to our thinking but endow the whole constellation with the majesty of the new reality, which may be neither new nor real. Reality is not necessarily that which happens to support the convenience of the moment. If we use it in that way we are acting as if we are twisting figures to fit our foregone conclusion.

Reality is not necessarily what gives us the way to voice our rationalizations and short-circuited proofs. Used as a wedge in our heel to correct a limp and give the appearance of walking straight, reality is merely another crutch. So many of our crutches balance each other and are not needed.

Imagination. Image. Vision. When we begin to see our dreams in our mind's eye, and when we imagine it with details and envision it in mental pictures, we give it dominion. In doing this, we are rewarded with third sight, that is, we convert ordinary vision into a creative potential. With our third sight we can then recognize the crutches that balance each other—and the ones we never needed at all.

List of Institutions Concerned with Psychic Phenomena

American Society for Psychical Research,
5 West 73rd Street
New York, New York 10023

Central Premonitions Registry,
P.O. Box 482,
Times Square Station
New York, New York 10036

Foundation for Mind Research (Robert Masters & Jean Houston),
Pomona, New York

Foundation for Research on the Nature of Man,
P.O. Box 6847
Durham, North Carolina 27708

Foundation for Psychic-Energetic Research, Ltd.,
250 East 63rd Street
New York, New York 10021

Information Research (publishes a directory),
90 Yardley Avenue
Toronto, Ontario, Canada

Lucis Trust Library,
866 United Nations Plaza,
New York, New York 10017

Maimonides Medical Center, Department of Psychiatry,
Division Parapsychology,
4802 Tenth Avenue,
Brooklyn, New York 11219

Menninger Foundation,
Topeka, Kansas

Mind Science Foundation,
San Antonio, Texas

Parapsychology Foundation,
29 West 57th Street,
New York, New York 10019

Premonitions Bureau, Toronto Society for Psychical Research,
10 North Sherbourne Street
Toronto, M4Y 2L8, Ontario, Canada

Premonitions Registry of Society for Psychic Research,
170 South Beverly Hills Drive
Beverly Hills, California 90212

Psychical Research Foundation,
Duke Station, Durham, North Carolina 27706

St. Joseph's College, Parapsychology Lab,
Philadelphia, Pennsylvania 19131

Spiritual Frontiers Fellowship,
10715 Winner Road,
Independence, Missouri 64052

University of Virginia, School of Medicine,
Division of Parapsychology,
Charlottesville, Virginia 22901

Reading List

BIOLOGICAL RHYTHM

Aschoff, J., "Circadian Systems in Man and their Implications."
Hospital Practice, May 1976.

Axelrod, Julius, *Endeavour,* Sept., 1970.
Science, 184; 1341; June 28, 1974.

Brown, F.A. Jr., *et al.,* *Am. J. Physiology.* 195; 237; 1958.

Burke, John F., "Timing Antibiotics to Prevent Infection."
Drug Therapy, Pilot Issue, 1975.

Focan, C., "Circadian Rhythm and Chemotherapy for Cancer."
The Laucet, Sept. 18, 1976.

Gittelson, Bernard, *Biorhythm—A Personal Science.*
Arco Publishing Company, New York,
(Paperback) 1976.
    and
Warner Books, New York, (Paperback)   1976.

Hemingway, Mary Welsh, *How It Was.*
Alfred E. Knopf, New York, 1976.

Halberg, Franz, *et al.*, *Perspectives in Biology and Medicine*, 17, 128; 1973.

Kaufman, Gerald K., *The Book of Time*. Julian Messner, New York, 1938.

Luce, Gay Gaer (Editor), *Biological Rhythms in Human and Animal Physiology*. Dover, New York, (Paperback) 1971.

Scheving, Lawrence D., "The Dimensions of Time in Biology and Medicine—Chronobiology." *Endeavour*, May 1976.

O'Neill, Barbara, and Richards, Phillip, *Biorhythms —How to Live with Your Life Cycles*. New American Library, New York (Paperback) 1975.

Weitzman, Elliot D., "Biological Rhythm and Hormone Secretion Pattern." *Hospital Practice*, Aug. 1976.

Zucker, Irving, "Light, Behavior and Biological Rhythm." *Hospital Practice*, Oct. 1976.

BUSINESS

Heller, Joseph, *Something Happened*. Knopf, New York 1974. Ballantine (Paperback) 1975.

Maccoby, Michael, *The Gamesman*. Simon & Schuster, New York, 1977.

Whyte, William H., Jr., *The Organization Man*. Simon & Schuster, New York, 1957.

CREATIVITY

Alfrey, Turner, Jr., "The Psychology of Invention in Chemistry, Physics and Mathematics." *Record. Chem. Progress*, 14; 191; 1953.

Arieti, Silvano, *Creativity—The Magic Synthesis*.
   Basic Books, Inc., New York, 1976.

Barthel, Joan, *A DEATH IN CANAAN*.
   E. P. Dutton, New York, 1976.

Chesterman, John, *et al.*, *AN INDEX OF POSSIBILITIES*
   —Energy and Power.
   Pantheon Books, New York (Paperback), 1974.

Clausewitz, Karl von, "On War"
   Infantry Journal Press, Washington, D.C., 1950.

Crawford, Robert P., *The Techniques of Creative Thinking. How to Use Your Ideas to Achieve Success*.
   Hawthorn Books, New York (Paperback), 1966.

De Bono, Edward, *PO: A Device for Successful Thinking*.
   Simon & Schuster, New York, 1972.

Dickson, Paul, *Think Tanks*.
   Ballantine Books, New York (Paperback), 1971.

Dubos, René, *Science*, 154; 595; Nov. 4, 1966.

Fearnside, W. Ward, and Holter, William B., *Fallacy—
   The Counterfeit of Argument*.
   Prentice-Hall, Englewood Cliffs, N.J.
   (Paperback), 1959.

Florman, Samuel C., *The Existential Pleasure of Engineering*. St. Martin's Press, New York, 1976.

Garrett, Alfred B., *The Flash of Genius*.
   D. Van Nostrand Co., Princeton, N.J., 1963.

Getzels, Jacob W., and Jackson, Philip W., *Creativity and
   Intelligence—Exploration with Gifted Students*.
   John Wiley & Sons, New York, 1962.

Ghiselin, Brewster (Editor), *The Creative Process*.
The New American Library, New York
(Paperback), 1952.

Gibson, William C., *Creative Minds in Medicine—Creative, Humanistic, and Cultural Contributions by Physicians*.
Charles C. Thomas, Springfield, Ill., 1963.

Gowan, John C., Demos, George D., and Torrance E. Paul, (Editors), *Creativity: Its Educational Implications*.
John Wiley & Sons, New York (Paperback), 1967.

Gregory, Carl E., *The Management of Intelligence—Scientific Problem Solving and Creativity*.
McGraw-Hill Book Co., New York, 1967.

Hadamard, Jacques, *The Psychology of Invention in the Mathematical Field*.
Princeton University Press, Princeton, N.J., 1945.

Harris, Harold (Editor), *Astride the Two Cultures—Arthur Koestler at 70*.
Random House, New York, 1976.

Kagan, Jerome (Editor), *Creativity and Learning*.
Beacon Press, Boston, Mass. (Paperback), 1967.

Koestler, Arthur, *The Act of Creation*.
The Macmillan Co., New York, 1967.
Dell, New York (Paperback) 1964.

Koestler, Arthur, *The Ghost in the Machine*.
The Macmillan Co., New York, 1967.

Koestler, Arthur, and Smythies. J. R. (Editors), *Beyond Reductionism—New Perspectives in the Life Sciences—The Alpbach Symposium*.
Beacon Press, Boston, Mass. (Paperback), 1969.

Kubie, Lawrence E., *Neurotic Distortion of the Creative Process.*
Farrar, Straus & Giroux, New York (Paperback), 1958.

Kuhn, Thomas S., *The Structure of Scientific Revolutions.*
University of Chicago Press, Chicago, Ill., 1970.

Leake, Chauncey D., *What Are We Living For?*
Practical Philosophy—Vol. 1. The Ethics
Vol. 2. The Logics
Vol. 3. The Aesthetics
PJD Publications, Ltd., Westbury, N.Y. 11590

Lowes, John Livingston, *The Road to Xanadu—A Study in the Ways of the Imagination.*
Vintage Books, New York (Paperback), 1959.

May, Rollo, *The Courage to Create.*
W. W. Norton, Co., New York, 1975.
Bantam, New York (Paperback), 1977.

Polya, George, *Mathematical Discovery—On Understanding, Learning, and Teaching Problem Solving.*
John Wiley & Sons, New York, 1962.

Rosen, Stephen. *Future Facts—The Way Things are Going to Work in the Future in Technology, Science, Medicine and Life.*
Simon & Schuster, New York, 1976.

Steig, William, *Dominic.*
Farrar, Strauss & Giroux, New York, 1972.

Tabori, Paul, *The Natural History of Stupidity.*
Chilton Co., Philadelphia, 1959.

Taylor, Calvin W., *Widening Horizons in Creativity.*
John Wiley & Sons, New York, 1964.

Taylor, Calvin W., and Barron, Frank (Editors), *Scientific Creativity—Its Recognition and Development.*
John Wiley & Sons, New York, 1963.

Thompson, W. F., "Open Doors to Serendipity."
Industrial Lab, March 1958.

Trench, Archbishop Richard C., *On the Study of Words.*
Sixteenth Edition, Macmillan, New York, 1876.

Turner, Joseph, *Science,* 126; 431; Sept. 6, 1957.

Unamuno, Miguel de, *Essays and Soliloquies.*
Alfred A. Knopf, New York, 1925.

Velikovsky, Immanuel, *Worlds in Collision.*
Delta, New York (Paperback), 1965.
Pocketbooks, New York (Paperback), 1977.

Vernon, P. E. (Editor), *Creativity.*
Penguin Books, Inc., New York (Paperback), 1970.

Weyl, Nathaniel, *The Creative Elite in America.*
Public Affairs Press, Washington, D.C., 1966.

Wilson, Colin, *The Strength to Dream—Literature and and the Imagination.*
Houghton, Mifflin & Co., Boston, 1962.

DREAMS

Garfield, Patricia, *Creative Dreaming.*
Ballantine Books, New York (Paperback), 1974.

Gumperz, Robert, *Dream Notebook—Notebook Toward Noting and Recollecting Dreams.*
San Francisco Book Co., San Francisco, Calif., 1976.

Ullman, Montague and Krippner, Stanley, *Dream Telepathy—Experiments in Nocturnal Sleep.*
Penguin Books, Inc., New York (Paperback), 1974.

MEDITATION—TM & OTHERWISE

Ayling, Keith, "What Meditation Can and Cannot Do for You."
Psychic World, Jan. 1977.

Benson, Herbert, The Relaxation Response.
William Morrow, New York, 1975.
Avon, New York (Paperback), 1976.

Benson Herbert, et al., "Continuous Measurement of Oxygen Consumption, and Carbon Dioxide Elimination During wakeful, Hypometabolic States."
J. Human Stress, 1; 37; Mar. 1975.

Ebon, Martin, TM—How to Find Peace of Mind Through Meditation.
New American Library, New York (Paperback), 1976.

Ebon, Martin, The Relaxation Controversy—Can You Have Relaxation Without Meditation?
New American Library, New York (Paperback), 1976.

Le Shan, Lawrence, How to Meditate—A Guide to Self-Discovery.
Bantam Books, New York (Paperback), 1975.

Michael, Richard P., Science 172; 964; 1974.

Wallace, Robert K., "Physiologic Effects of TM."
Science 167; 1751; Mar. 27, 1970.
"TM: Meditation or Sleep?"
Science 193; 000; Aug. 27, 1976.

MEMORY & BOREDOM

Anon., Instant Memory Book.
Institute of Advanced Thinking 845 Via de la Paz, Pacific Palisades, Cal. 90272, 1972.

Cermak, Laird S., *Improving Your Memory*.
McGraw-Hill, New York (Paperback), 1977.

Grossmith, George, and Grossmith, Weedon, *The Diary of a Nobody*. Collins, London, 1894.

Heron, Woodburn, "The Pathology of Boredom."
Scientific American, Jan. 1957.

Lorayne, Harry, and Lucas, Jerry, *The Memory Book*.
Stein & Day, New York, 1974.

Young, Morris N., and Gibson, Walter B., *How to Develop An Exceptional Memory*.
Wilshire Book Co., North Hollywood, Calif.
(Paperback), 1962.

MIND & BEHAVIOR

Adam, Michael, *Wandering in Eden—Three Ways to the East Within Us*.
Alfred A. Knopf, New York (Paperback), 1976.

Baker, Elsworth F., *Man in the Trap—The Causes of Blocked Sexual Energy*.
Avon Books, New York (Paperback), 1967.

Brown, Barbara B., *New Mind, New Body—Biofeedback: New Directions for the Mind*.
Bantam Books, New York (Paperback), 1975.

Buzan, Tony, *Use Both Sides of your Brain, Techniques to Help you read Efficiently, Study Effectively, Solve Problems, Remember More, Think Creatively*.
E. P. Dutton & Co., New York (Paperback), 1976.

Cohn, Norman, *Europe's Inner Demons—An Enquiry Inspired by the Great Witch-Hunt*.
Basic Books, New York, 1975.

Cohn Norman, *The Pursuit of the Millennium. Revolutionary Millenarians and Mystical Anarchists of the Middle Ages.*
Oxford University Press, New York (Paperback), 1970.

Edinger, Edward F., *Ego and Archetype—A Synthesis of Jung's Psychological Concepts—Individuation and the Religious Function of the Psyche.*
Penguin Books, New York (Paperback), 1972.

Ferguson, Marilyn, *The Brain Revolution—The Frontiers of Mind Research.*
Taplinger Publishing Co., New York, 1973.
Bantam Books, New York (Paperback), 1974.

Grof, Stanislav, *Realms of the Human Unconscious—Observations from LSD Research.*
E. P. Dutton & Co., New York (Paperback), 1976.

Harding, M. Esther, *Psychic Energy—Its Source and Goal.*
Pantheon Books, New York, 1948.

Jonas, Gerald, *Visceral Learning.*
The Viking Press, New York, 1973.

Jung, Carl G., *Answer to Job.*
Meridian Books, New York (Paperback), 1960.

Jung, Carl G. *The Undiscovered Self—Closing the Widening Gulf Between the Conscious and Unconscious Aspects of the Human Psyche.*
New American Library, New York (Paperback), 1957.

Lowen, Alexander, *Bioenergetics—The Language of the Body to Heal the Problems of the Mind.*
Penguin Books, New York (Paperback), 1975.

Mishlove, Jeffrey, *The Roots of Consciousness—Psychic Liberation Through History, Science and Experience.*
Random House, New York (Paperback), 1975.

Needleman, Jacob and Lewis, Dennis (Editors), *Sacred Tradition and Present Need.*
The Viking Press, New York, 1975.

O'Connell, Margaret F., *The Magic Cauldron—Witchcraft for Good and Evil.*
S. G. Phillips, Inc., New York, 1975.

Ostrander, Sheila, and Schroeder, Lynn, *Psychic Discoveries Behind the Iron Curtain.*
Bantam Books, New York (Paperback), 1971.

Samuels, Mike, and Samuels, Nancy, *Seeing with the Mind's Eye—History, Techniques, and Uses of Visualization.*
Random House, New York (Paperback), 1975.

Scarf, Maggie, *Body, Mind, Behavior.*
New Republic Book Co., Washington, D.C., 1976.

Torrey, E. Fuller, *The Mind Game—Witch Doctors and Psychiatrists.*
Bantam Books, New York (Paperback), 1973.
"Witch Doctors and Other Psychiatrists."
Medical Opinion, Aug. 1971.

Waldo-Schwartz, Paul, *Art and the Occult.*
Paul Braziller, New York (Paperback), 1975.

MYTHS & FOLKLORE

Campbell, Joseph, *The Masks of God: Creative Mythology.*
Penguin Books (Paperback), New York, 1968.

Fischer, Martin (Editor), *Gracian's Manual—The Truthtelling Manual and the Art of Worldly Wisdom of Baltasar Gracian, (1653).*
Charles C. Thomas, Springfield, Ill., 1945.

Majno, Guido,   *The Healing Hand—Man and Wound in the Ancient World.*
Harvard University Press, Cambridge, Mass., 1975.

Nicholas, Marianne,   *Man, Myth, and Monument.*
William Morrow & Co., New York (Paperback), 1975.

Santillana, Giorgio de, and von Dechend, Hertha, *Hamlet's Mill—An Essay on Myth and the Frame of Time. A Journey Back Through Time to the Origins of Human Knowledge in the Preliterate World.*
Gambit, Inc., Boston, Mass. 02108, 1969.

PSYCHIC, OCCULT & SPIRITUAL SEARCHING

American Medical Association,   *Today's Health,* Oct. 1971.

Boyer, Paul and Nissenbaum, Stephen,   *Salem Possessed—The Social Origins of Witchcraft.*
Harvard University Press, Cambridge, Mass., 1974.

Burr, Harold S.,   *The Fields of Life—Our Links with the Universe.*
Ballantine Books, New York (Paperback), 1972.

Chaplin, J. P.,   *Dictionary of the Occult and Paranormal.*
Dell, New York (Paperback), 1976.

Cox, Harvey,   *The Seduction of the Spirit—The Use and Misuse of People's Religion.*
Simon & Schuster, New York, 1973.

Ebon, Martin,   *The Psychic Scene—Explorations into Telepathy, Psychic Phenomena, Mysticism, The Life Beyond, Reincarnation.*
New American Library, New York (Paperback), 1974.

Ebon, Maiter, *What's New in ESP.*
Pyramid Books, New York (Paperback), 1976.

Fuller, John G.,   *Arigo—Surgeon of the Rusty Knife*.
Pocket Books, New York (Paperback), 1975.

Kramer, Heinrich, and Sprenger, James,   *The Malleus Maleficarum—The Witches' Hammer*.
Dover Publications, New York (Paperback), 1971.

Law, Donald,   *A Guide to Alternative Medicine—An Examination of Sixty Different Forms of Healing from Auras to Herbalism*.
Doubleday, New York (Paperback), 1976.

Le Shan, Lawrence,   *The Medium, the Mystic, and the Physicist—Toward a General Theory of the Paranormal*.
The Viking Press, New York, 1976.

Lilly, John C.,   *Simulations of God—The Science of Belief*.
Bantam Books, New York (Paperback), 1975.

Mitchell, Edgar D.,   *Psychic Exploration—A Challenge for Science*.
G. P. Putnam's Sons, New York, 1974.

Messegué, Maurice,   *Of Men and Plants—Autobiography of the Famous Plant Healer*.
Bantam Books, New York (Paperback), 1974.

Moore, Clara Bloomfield,   *Keeley and His Discoveries*.
University Books, Secaucus, N.J.

Moss, Thelma,   *The Probability of the Unconscious—Scientific Discoveries and Explorations in the Psychic World*.
J. P. Tarcher, Los Angeles, Calif., 1974.

Needleman, Jacob, *A Sense of the Cosmos—The Encounter of Modern Science and Ancient Truth*.
Doubleday, New York (Paperback), 1976.

Neugroschel, Joachim (Editor),   *Jenne Welt—The Great Works of Jewish Fantasy and Occult*. (2 Volumes.) Stonehill Publishing Co., New York, 1976.

Ostrander, Sheila, and Schroeder, Lynn,   *The ESP Papers —Scientists Speak out from Beyond the Iron Curtain*. Bantam Books, New York (Paperback), 1976.

Panati, Charles,   *Supersenses—Our Potential for Parasensory Experiences*. Quadrangle, New York, 1974.

Pearce, Joseph Chilton,   *The Crack in the Cosmic Egg— Challenging the Costructs of Mind and Reality*. Pocket Books, New York (Paperback), 1973.

Exploring the Crack in the Cosmic Egg—An Investigation of Non-Ordinary Reality; Split Minds and Metarealities. Pocket Books, New York (Paperback), 1975.

Raudive, Konstantin,   *Breakthrough—Experiment in Electronic Communication with the Dead*. Taplinger Publishing Co., New York, 1971.

Roberts, Jane,   *The Coming of Seth—A Day-by-Day Record of Psychic Experiences*. Pocket Books, New York (Paperback), 1976.

Shealy, C. Norman,   *Occult Medicine Can Save Your Life —A Modern Doctor Looks at Unconventional Healing*. The Dial Press, New York, 1975.

Smith, Adam,   *Powers of the Mind*. Random House, New York, 1975. Ballantine, New York (Paperback), 1976.

Tralins, Robert,   *Supernatural Warnings*. Popular Library, New York (Paperback), 1974.

Watson, Lyall, *Supernature—An Unprecedented Look at Strange Phenomena and Their Place in Nature.* Anchor Press-Doubleday, New York, 1973.

Woods, William, *A Casebook for Witchcraft.* G. P. Putnam's Sons, New York, 1974.

PSYCHOLOGY, PHILOSOPHY, RELIGION

Bakewell, Charles M., *Sourcebook in Ancient Philosophy.* Scribner, New York, 1939.

Bromley, D. B., *The Psychology of Human Ageing.* Penguin Books, New York (Paperback), 1974.

Brown, Rosellen, *Autobiography of my Mother.* Doubleday, New York, 1976.

Coles, Robert, *The Mind's Fate—Ways of Seeing Psychiatry and Psychoanalysis.* Little, Brown & Co., Boston (Paperback), 1975.

De Reuck, A. V. S., and Porter, Ruth, (Editors), *Transcultural Psychiatry.* Little, Brown & Co., Boston, Mass., 1965.

Ennis, Bruce J., *Prisoners of Psychiatry—Mental Patients, Psychiatrists and the Law.* Avon Books, New York (Paperback), 1972.

Garn, Roy, *The Magic Power of Emotional Appeal.* Ace Books (Paperback), 1960.

Gombrich, E. H., *Art and Illusion—A Study in the Psychology of Pictorial Representation.* Priceton University Press, Princeton, N.J. (Paperback), 1969.

James, Fleming, *Personalities of the Old Testament.* Scribners, New York, 1939.

James, William, *The Varieties of Religious Experience—A Study in Human Nature.*
New American Library, New York (Paperback), 1958.

Le Bon, Gustave, *The Crowd—A Study of the Popular Mind.*
Ballantine Books, New York (Paperback), 1969.

Needleman, Jacob, and Lewis, Dennis (Editors), *On The Way to Self-Knowledge—The Aims and Disciplines of Sacred Tradition and Psychotherapy.*
Alfred A. Knopf, New York (Paperback) 1976.

Olson, Ken, *The Art of Hanging Loose in An Uptight World—Psychological Exercises for Personal Growth.*
Fawcett Publications, Greenwich, Conn.
(Paperback), 1974.

Orford, Jim, *The Social Psychology of Mental Disorder.*
Penguin-Viking, New York (Paperback), 1976.

Ornstein, R. E., *The Psychology of Consciousness.*
Penguin Book, Inc., New York (Paperback), 1972.

Tennov, Dorothy, *Psychotherapy—The Hazardous Cure.*
Doubleday, New York (Paperback), 1976.

Walker, Williston, *A History of the Christian Church.*
Scribners, New York, 1959.

Würthwein, Ernst, *The Text of the Old Testament.*
Macmillan, New York, 1957.

SCIENCE

Bennett, André M., "Science: The Antithesis of Creativity."
Perspectives in Biology and Medicine, 11; 233; Winter 1968.

Cohen, Harry, and Cormin, I. J. (Editors),   *Jews in the World of Science.*
Monde Publishers, New York, 1956.

Davis, Frederick H.,   "Patterns in the Distortion of the Scientific Method."
Southern Medical Journal, Sept. 1960.

Lewin, Roger,   *In Defense of the Body—An Introduction to the New Immunology.*
Doubleday, New York (Paperback), 1974.

Mendelson, Everett I.,   *Time Magazine,* April 23, 1973.

STRESS & COPING

Brown, Barbara B.,   *Stress and the Art of Biofeedback.*
Harper & Row, New York, 1977.

Caruthers, Malcolm, *et al., Lancet,* 1; 997; 1976.

Day, G.,   *Lancet,* 1; 666; 1951.

Friedman, Meyer, and Rosenman, Ray H.,   *Type A Behavior and Your Heart.*
Knopf, New York, 1974.
Fawcett, New York (Paperback), 1975.

Grossman, Milton S.,   *World Medical News,* Jan. 26, 1965.

Hardy, James D.,   *'Surgery, Gynecology and Obstetrics',*
108; 368; March 1959.

Henry, James P., *et al., Psychosomatic Medicine,* 29; 408; 1967.

Holmes, Thomas S., and Holmes, T. H., "Stress"
Continuing Education for Family Physicians
May 1975.
Med. Book Club, Kansas City, Missouri 64112.

Holmes, T. H., and Rahe, R. H.,   *Journal Psychosomatic Research,* 11; 213; 1967.

Lamott, Kenneth,   *Escape from Stress—Learning Relaxation with the Right Response.*
Berkley Publishing Corp., New York (Paperback), 1975.

Lazarus, Richard S.,   *Psychological Stress and the Coping Process.*
McGraw-Hill Book Co., New York, 1966.

Perla, David, and Marmorston, Jessie,   *Natural Resistance and Clinical Medicine.*
Little, Brown & Co., Boston, 1954.

Selye, Hans,   *Stress Without Distress—How to Use Stress as a Positive Force to Achieve a Rewarding Life Style.*
New American Library, New York (Paperback), 1974.
Nutrition Today, Spring 1970.

Silverman, Samuel,   *Psychological Aspects of Physical Symptoms.*
Appleton-Century-Crofts, New York, 1967.

Index

251